George Long

Meditations of Marcus Aurelius Antoninus, Emperor of the Romans

George Long

Meditations of Marcus Aurelius Antoninus, Emperor of the Romans

ISBN/EAN: 9783337037987

Printed in Europe, USA, Canada, Australia, Japan

Cover: Foto ©Suzi / pixelio.de

More available books at **www.hansebooks.com**

Meditations

OF

Marcus Aurelius Antoninus

EMPEROR OF THE ROMANS

TRANSLATED BY GEORGE LONG

NEW AND COMPLETE EDITION

CHICAGO :
CORNELIUS H. SHAVER,
MDCCCLXXXII:

To

RALPH WALDO EMERSON,

THIS EDITION OF

THE THOUGHTS OF. THE EMPEROR M. AURELIUS
ANTONINUS,

IS INSCRIBED BY THE PUBLISHERS.

CONTENTS.

The portrait of Marcus Aurelius Antoninus is from a bust in the British Museum. The medallion die is from a coin of the time of Aurelius.

M. AURELIUS ANTONINUS.

M. ANTONINUS was born at Rome A. D. 121, on the 26th of April. His father Annius Verus died while he was praetor. His mother was Domitia Calvilla, also named Lucilla. The Emperor Antoninus Pius married Annia Galeria Faustina, the sister of Annius Verus, and was consequently Antoninus' uncle. When Hadrian adopted Antoninus Pius and declared him his successor in the empire, Antoninus Pius adopted both L. Ceionius Commodus, the son of Aelius Caesar, and M. Antoninus, whose original name was M. Annius Verus. Antoninus took the name of M. Aelius Aurelius Verus, to which was added the title of Caesar in A. D. 139 : the name Aelius belonged to Hadrian's family, and Aurelius was the name of Antoninus Pius. When M. Antoninus became Augustus, he dropped the name of Verus and took the name of Antoninus. Accordingly he is generally named M. Aurelius Antoninus, or simply M. Antoninus.

The youth was most carefully brought up. He thanks the gods (I. 17) that he had good grandfathers, good parents, a good sister, good teachers,

good associates, good kinsmen and friends, nearly
everything good.   He had the happy fortune to
witness the example of his uncle and adoptive .
father Antoninus Pius, and he has recorded in
his work (I. 16 ; VI. 30) the virtues of this excellent man and prudent ruler.   Like many young
Romans he tried his hand at poetry and studied
rhetoric.   Herodes Atticus and M. Cornelius
Fronto were his teachers in eloquence.   There
are extant letters between Fronto and Marcus,
which show the great affection of the pupil for
the master, and the master's great hopes of his in-
dustrious pupil.   M. Antoninus mentions Fronto
(I. 11) among those to whom he was indebted for
his education.

When he was eleven years old, he assumed the
dress of philosophers, something plain and coarse,
became a hard student, and lived a most laborious abstemious life, even so far as to injure his
health.   Finally, he abandoned poetry and rhetoric for philosophy, and he attached himself to
the sect of the Stoics.   But he did not neglect
the study of law, which was a useful preparation
for the high place which he was designed to fill.
His teacher was L. Volusianus Maecianus, a distinguished jurist.   We must suppose that he
learned the Roman discipline of arms, which was
a necessary part of the education of a man who
afterwards led his troops to battle against a war-
like race.

Antoninus has recorded in his first book the
names of his teachers and the obligations which

he owed to each of them. The way in which
he speaks of what he learned from them might
seem to savor of vanity or self-praise, if we look
carelessly at the way in which he has expressed
himself; but if any one draws this conclusion, he
will be mistaken. Antoninus means to commemorate the merits of his several teachers, what
they taught and what a pupil might learn from
them. Besides, this book like the eleven other
books, was for his own use, and if we may trust
the note at the end of the first book, it was written during one of M. Antoninus' campaigns against
the Quadi, at a time when the commemoration of
the virtues of his illustrious teachers might remind him of their lessons and the practical uses
which he might derive from them.

Among his teachers of philosophy was Sextus
of Chaeroneia, a grandson of Plutarch. What
he learned from this excellent man is told by himself (I. 9). His favorite teacher was Q. Junius
Rusticus (I. 7), a philosopher and also a man of
practical good sense in public affairs. Rusticus
was the adviser of Antoninus after he became
emperor. Young men who are destined for high
places are not often fortunate in those who are
about them, their companions and teachers; and
I do not know any example of a young prince
having had an education which can be compared
with that of M. Antoninus. Such a body of
teachers distinguished by their acquirements and
their character will hardly be collected again; and
as to the pupil, we have not had one like him since.

Hadrian died in July A. D. 138, and was succeeded by Antoninus Pius. M. Antoninus married Faustina, his cousin, the daughter of Pius, probably about A. D. 146, for he had a daughter born in 147. M. Antoninus received from his adoptive father the title of Caesar and was associated with him in the administration of the state. The father and the adopted son lived together in perfect friendship and confidence. Antoninus was a dutiful son, and the emperor Pius loved and esteemed him.

Antoninus Pius died in March 161. The Senate, it is said, urged M. Antoninus to take the solemn administration of the empire, but he associated with himself the other adopted son of Pius, L. Ceionius Commodus, who is generally called L. Verus. Thus Rome for the first time had two emperors. Verus was an indolent man of pleasure and unworthy of his station. Antoninus however bore with him, and it is said that Verus had sense enough to pay to his colleague the respect due to his character. A virtuous emperor and a loose partner lived together in peace, and their alliance was strengthened by Antoninus giving to Verus for wife his daughter Lucilla.

The reign of Antoninus was first troubled by a Parthian war, in which Verus was sent to command, but he did nothing, and the success that was obtained by the Romans in Armenia and on the Euphrates and Tigris was due to his generals. This Parthian war ended in 165.

The north of Italy was also threatened by the rude people beyond the Alps from the borders of Gallia to the eastern side of the Hadriatic. These barbarians attempted to break into Italy, as the Germanic nations had attempted near three hundred years before; and the rest of the life of Antoninus with some intervals was employed in driving back the invaders. In 169 Verus suddenly died, and Antoninus administered the state alone.

In A. D. 175 Avidius Cassius, a brave and skilful Roman commander who was at the head of the troops in Asia, revolted and declared himself Augustus. But Cassius was assassinated by some of his officers, and so the rebellion came to an end. Antoninus showed his humanity by his treatment of the family and the partisans of Cassius, and his letter to the senate in which he recommends mercy is extant. (Vulcatius, Avidius Cassius, c. 12.)

Antoninus set out for the east on hearing of Cassius' revolt. We know that in A. D. 174 he was engaged in a war against the Quadi, Marcomanni and other Germanic tribes, and it is probable that he went direct from the German war without returning to Rome. His wife Faustina who accompanied him into Asia died suddenly at the foot of the Taurus to the great grief of her husband. Capitolinus who has written the life of Antoninus, and also Dion Cassius accuse the empress of scandalous infidelity to her husband and of abominable lewdness. But Capitolinus says that Antoninus either knew it not or pretended not to know it. Nothing is so common as such malicious reports in all ages, and the history of imperial Rome is full of them. Antoninus loved his wife and he says that she was "obedient, affectionate, and simple." The same scandal had been spread about Faustina's mother, the wife of Antoninus Pius, and yet he too was perfectly satisfied with his wife. Antoninus Pius says in a letter to Fronto that he would rather live in exile with his wife than in his palace at Rome without her. There are not many men who would give their wives a better character than these two emperors. Capitolinus wrote in the time of Diocletian. He may have intended to tell the truth, but he is a poor, feeble biographer. Dion Cassius, the most malignant of historians, always reports and perhaps he believed any scandal against anybody.

Antoninus continued his journey to Syria and Egypt, and on his return to Italy through Athens he was initiated into the Eleusinian mysteries. It was the practice of the emperor to conform to the established rites of the age and to perform religious ceremonies with due solemnity. We cannot conclude from this that he was a superstitious man, though we might perhaps do so, if his book did not show that he was not. But this is only one among many instances that a ruler's public acts do not always prove his real opinions. A prudent governor will not roughly oppose even the superstitions of his people, and though he may wish that they were wiser, he will know that he cannot make them so by offending their prejudices.

Antoninus and his son Commodus entered Rome in triumph on the 23rd of December A. D. 176. In the following year Commodus was associated with his father in the empire and took the name of Augustus. This year A. D. 177 is memorable in ecclesiastical history. Attalus and others were put to death at Lyon for their adherence to the Christian religion. The evidence of this persecution is a letter preserved by Eusebius (E. H. v. 1; printed in Routh's Reliquiae Sacrae, vol. I. with notes). The letter is from the Christians of Vienna and Lugdunum in Gallia (Vienne and Lyon) to their Christian brethren in Asia and Phrygia; and it is preserved perhaps nearly entire. It contains a very particular description of the tortures inflicted on the Christians in Gallia, and it states that while the persecution was going on, Attalus a Christian and a Roman citizen was loudly demanded by the populace and brought into the amphitheatre, but the governor ordered him to be reserved with the rest who were in prison, until he had received instructions from the emperor. It is not clear who the " rest "- were who are mentioned in the letter. Many had been tortured before the governor thought of applying to the emperor. The imperial rescript, says the letter, was that the Christians should be punished, but if they would deny their faith, they must be released. On this the work began again.

The Christians who were Roman citizens were beheaded: the rest were exposed to the wild beasts in the amphitheatre. Some modern writers on ecclesiastical history, when they use this letter, say nothing of the wonderful stories of the martyrs' sufferings. Sanctus, as the letter says, was burnt with plates of hot iron till his body was one sore and had lost all human form, but on being put to the rack he recovered his former appearance under the torture, which was thus a cure instead of a punishment. He was afterwards torn by beasts, and placed on an iron chair and roasted. He died at last.

The letter is one piece of evidence. The writer, whoever he was that wrote in the name of the Gallic Christians, is our evidence both for the ordinary and the extraordinary circumstances of the story, and we cannot accept his evidence for one part and reject the other. We often receive small evidence as proof of a thing which we believe to be within the limits of probability or possibility, and we reject exactly the same evidence, when the thing to which it refers, appears very improbable or impossible. But this is a false method of inquiry, though it is followed by some modern writers, who select what they like from a story and reject the rest of the evidence; or if they do not reject it, they dishonestly suppress it. A man can only act consistently by accepting all this letter or rejecting it all, and we cannot blame him for either. But he who rejects it may still admit that such a letter may be founded on real facts ; and he would make this admission as the most probable way of accounting for the existence of the letter : but if, as he would suppose, the writer has stated some things falsely, he cannot tell what part of his story is worthy of credit.

The war on the northern frontier appears to have been uninterrupted during the visit of Antoninus to the East, and on his return the emperor again left Rome to oppose the barbarians. The Germanic people were defeated in a great battle A. D. 179. During this campaign the emperor was seized with some contagious malady, of which he died in the camp at Sirmium (Mitrovitz) on the Save in Lower Pannonia, but at Vindebona (Vienna) according to other authorities, on the 17th of March A. D. 180, in the fifty-ninth year of his age. His son Commodus was with him. His body, or the ashes probably, was carried to Rome, and he received the honor of deification. Those who could afford it had his statue or bust, and when Capitolinus wrote, many people still had statues of Antoninus among the Dei Penates or household deities. He was in a manner made a saint. His son Commodus erected to his memory the Antonine column which is now in the Piazza Colonna at Rome. The bassi rilievi which are placed in a spiral line round the shaft commemorate his father's victories over the Marcomanni and the Quadi, and the miraculous shower of rain which refreshed the Roman soldiers and discomfited their enemies. The statue of Antoninus was placed on the column, but it was removed at some time unknown, and a bronze statue of St. Paul was put in its place by Pope Sixtus the fifth.

The historical evidence for the times of Antoninus is very defective, and some of that which remains is not credible. The most curious is the story about the miracle which happened in A. D. 174 during the war with the Quadi. The Roman army was in danger of perishing by thirst, but a sudden storm drenched them with rain, while it discharged fire and hail on their enemies, and the Romans gained a great victory. All the authorities which speak of the battle speak also of the miracle. The Gentile writers assign it to their gods, and the Christians to the intercession of the Christian legion in the emperor's army. To confirm the Christian statement it is added that the emperor gave the title of Thundering to this legion ; but Dacier and others who maintain the Christian report of the miracle, admit that this title of Thundering or Lightning was not given to this legion because the Quadi were struck with lightning, but because there was a figure of lightning on their shields, and that this title of the legion existed in he time of Augustus.

Scaliger also had observed that the legion was called Thundering (κεραυγοβόλος, or κεραυνοφόρος) before the reign of Antoninus. We learn this from Dion Cassius (Lib. 55, c. 23, and the note of Reimarus) who enumerates all the legions of Augustus' time. The name Thundering or Lightning also occurs on an inscription of the reign of Trajan, which was found at Trieste. Eusebius

(v. 5) when he relates the miracle, quotes Apolinarius, bishop of Hierapolis, as authority for this name being given to the legion Melitene by the emperor in consequence of the success which he obtained through their prayers ; from which we may estimate the value of Apolinarius' testimony. Eusebius does not say in what book of Apolinarius the statement occurs. Dion says that the Thundering legion was stationed in Cappadocia in the time of Augustus. Valesius also observes that in the Notitia of the Imperium Romanum there is mentioned under the commander of Armenia the Praefectura of the twelfth legion named "Thundering Melitene ;" and this position in Armenia will agree with what Dion says of its position in Cappadocia. Accordingly Valesius concludes that Melitene was not the name of the legion, but of the town in which it was stationed. The legions did not, he says, take their name from the place where they were on duty, but from the country in which they were raised, and therefore, what Eusebius says about the Melitene does not seem probable to him. Yet Valesius on the authority of Apolinarius and Tertullian believed that the miracle was worked through the prayers of the Christian soldiers in the emperor's army. Rufinus does not give the name of Melitene to this legion, says Valesius, and probably he purposely omitted it, because he knew that Melitene was the name of a town in Armenia Minor, where the legion was stationed in his time.

The emperor, it is said, made a report of his
2

victory to the Senate, which we may believe, for
such was the practice; but we do not know what
he said in his letter, for it is not extant.   Dacier
assumes that the emperor's letter was purposely
destroyed by the Senate or the enemies of Christianity, that so honorable a testimony to the
Christians and their religion might not be perpet-
uated.   The critic has however not seen that he
contradicts himself when he tells us the purport
of the letter, for he says that it was destroyed,
and even Eusebius could not find it.   But there
does exist a letter in Greek addressed by Antoninus to the Roman Senate after this memorable
victory.   It is sometimes printed after Justin's
second Apology, though it is totally unconnected
with the apologies.   This letter is one of the
most stupid forgeries of the many which exist,
and it cannot be possibly founded even on the
genuine report of Antoninus to the Senate.   If
it were genuine, it would free the emperor from
the charge of persecuting men because they were
Christians, for he says in this false letter that if
a man accuse another only of being a Christian
and the accused confess and there is nothing else
against him, he must be set free ; with this mon-
strous addition made by a man inconceivably ignorant, that the informer must be burnt alive.[1]

---

[1] Eusebius (v. 5) quotes Tertullian's Apology to the
Roman Senate in confirmation of the story.   Tertullian,
he says, writes that letters of the emperor were extant,
in which he declares that his army was saved by the
prayers of the Christians ; and that he " threatened to
punish with death those who ventured to accuse us."

During the time of Antoninus Pius and Marcus Antoninus there appeared the first Apology of Justinus, and under M. Antoninus the Oration of Tatian against the Greeks, which was a fierce attack on the established religions, the address of Athenagoras to M. Antoninus on behalf of the Christians, and the Apology of Melito, bishop of Sardes, also addressed to the emperor, and that of Apolinarius. The first Apology of Justinus is addressed to Antoninus Pius and his two adopted sons M. Antoninus and L. Verus ; but we do not know whether they read it. The second Apology of Justinus is addressed to the Roman Senate, but there is nothing in it which shows its date. In one passage where he is speaking of the persecution of the Christians, Justinus says that even men who followed the Stoic doctrines, when they ordered their lives according to ethical reason, were hated and murdered, such as Heraclitus, Musonius in his own times and others ; for all those who in any way labored to live according to reason and avoided wickedness were always hated ; and this was the effect of the work of daemons.

Justinus himself is said to have been put to death at Rome, because he refused to sacrifice to the gods ; but the circumstances of his death are doubtful, and the time is uncertain. It cannot

It is possible that the forged letter which is now extant may be one of those which Tertullian had seen, for he uses the plural number "letters." A great deal has been written about this miracle of the Thundering Legion, and more than is worth reading.

have been in the reign of Hadrian, as one authority states; nor in the time of Antoninus Pius,
if the second Apology was written in the time of
M. Antoninus.

The persecution in which Polycarp suffered at
Smyrna belongs to the time of M. Antoninus.
The evidence for it is the letter of the church
of Smyrna to the churches of Philomelium and
the other Christian churches, and it is preserved
by Eusebius (E. H. IV. 15). But the critics do
not agree about the time of Polycarp's death,
differing in the two extremes to the amount of
twelve years. The circumstances of Polycarp's
martyrdom were accompanied by miracles, one of
which Eusebius (IV. 15) has omitted, but it appears in the oldest Latin version of the letter,
which Usher published, and it is supposed that
this version was made not long after the time of
Eusebius. The notice at the end of the letter
states that it was transcribed by Caius from the
copy of Irenaeus, the disciple of Polycarp, then
transcribed by Socrates at Corinth; "after which
I Pionius again wrote it out from the copy above
mentioned, having searched it out by the revela-
tion of Polycarp, who directed me to it," &c. The
story of Polycarp's martyrdom is embellished with
miraculous circumstances which some modern
writers on ecclesiastical history take the liberty
of omitting.[2]

[2] Conyers Middleton, An Inquiry into the Miraculous Powers, &c. p. 126. Middleton says that Eusebius
omitted to mention the dove, which flew out of Poly-

In order to form a proper notion of the condition of the Christians under M. Antoninus we must go back to Trajan's time. When the younger Pliny was governor of Bithynia, the Christians were numerous in those parts, and the worshippers of the old religion were falling off. The temples were deserted, the festivals neglected, and there were no purchasers of victims for sacrifice. Those who were interested in the maintenance of the old religion thus found that their profits were in danger. Christians of both sexes and of all ages were brought before the governor, who did not know what to do with them. He could come to no other conclusion than this, that those who confessed to be Christians and persevered in their religion ought to be punished; if for nothing else, for their invincible obstinacy. He found no crimes proved against the Christians, and he could only characterize their religion as a depraved and extravagant superstition, which might be stopped, if the people were allowed the opportunity of recanting. Pliny wrote this in a letter to Trajan (Plinius, Ep. x. 97). He asked for the emperor's directions, because he did not know what to do: He remarks that he had never been engaged in judicial inquiries about

carp's body, and Dodwell and Archbishop Wake have done the same. Wake says, " I am so little a friend to such miracles that I thought it better with Eusebius to omit that circumstance than to mention it from Bishop Usher's Manuscript," which manuscript however, says Middleton, he afterwards declares to be so well attested that we need not any further assurance of the truth of it.

the Christians, and that accordingly he did not
know what or how far to inquire and punish.
This proves that it was not a new thing to inquire
into a man's profession of Christianity and to
punish him for it. Trajan's Rescript is extant.
He approved of the governor's judgment in the
matter; but he said that no search must be made
after the Christians; if a man was charged with
the new religion and convicted, he must not be
punished, if he affirmed that he was not a Christian and confirmed his denial by showing his reverence to the heathen gods. He added that no
notice must be taken of anonymous informations,
for such things were of bad example. Trajan
was a mild and sensible man, and both motives
of mercy and policy probably also induced him to
take as little notice of the Christians as he could;
to let them live in quiet, if it were possible.
Trajan's Rescript is the first legislative act of the
head of the Roman state with reference to Christianity, which is known to us. It does not appear
that the Christians were further disturbed under
his reign. The martyrdom of Ignatius by the
order of Trajan himself is not universally admitted to be an historical fact.

In the time of Hadrian it was no longer possible for the Roman government to overlook the
great increase of the Christians and the hostility
of the common sort to them. If the governors
in the provinces wished to let them alone, they
could not resist the fanaticism of the heathen
community, who looked on the Christians as athe-

ists. The Jews too who were settled all over the
Roman Empire were as hostile to the Christians
as the Gentiles were. With the time of Hadrian
begin the Christian Apologies, which show plainly
what the popular feeling towards the Christians
then was. A rescript of Hadrian to the Pro-
consul of Asia, which stands at the end of Justin's first apology, instructs the governor that
innocent people must not be troubled and false
accusers must not be allowed to extort money
from them ; the charges against the Christians
must be made in due form and no attention must
be paid to popular clamors ; when Christians
were regularly prosecuted and convicted of any
illegal act, they must be punished according to
their deserts ; and false accusers also must be punished. Antoninus Pius is said to have published
Rescripts to the same effect. The terms of Hadrian's Rescript seem very favorable to the
Christians, but if we understand it in this sense,
that they were only to be punished like other
people for illegal acts, it would have had no meaning, for that could have been done without asking
the emperor's advice. The real purpose of the
Rescript is that Christians must be punished if
they persisted in their belief, and would not prove
their renunciation of it by acknowledging the
heathen religion. This was Trajan's rule, and we
have no reason for supposing that Hadrian granted
more to the Christians than Trajan did. There
is printed at the end of Justin's Apology a Rescript of Antoninus Pius to the Commune of Asia

(τὸ κοινὸν τῆς Ἀσίας), and it is also in Eusebius [3]
(E. H. IV. 13). The Rescript declares that
the Christians, for they are meant, though the
name Christians does not occur in the Rescript,
were not to be disturbed, unless they were attempting something against the Roman rule, and no
man was to be punished simply for being a Christian. But this Rescript is spurious. Any man
moderately acquainted with Roman history will
see at once from the style and tenor that it is a
clumsy forgery.

In the time of M. Antoninus the opposition
between the old and the new belief was still
stronger, and the adherents of the heathen religion urged those in authority to a more regular
resistance to the invasions of the Christian faith.
Melito in his apology to M. Antoninus represents
the Christians of Asia as persecuted under new
imperial orders. Shameless informers, he says,
men who were greedy after the property of others,
used these orders as a means of robbing those who

[3] In Eusebius the name at the beginning of the Rescript is that of M. Antoninus ; and so we cannot tell to
which of the two emperors the forger assigned the Rescript. There are also a few verbal differences.

The author of the Alexandrine Chronicum says that
Marcus being moved by the entreaties of Melito and
other heads of the church wrote an Epistle to the Commune of Asia in which he forbade the Christians to be
troubled on account of their religion. Valesius supposes this to be the letter which is contained in Eusebius
(IV. 13), and to be the answer to the apology of Melito
of which I shall soon give the substance. But Marcus
certainly did not write this letter which is in Eusebius,
and we know not what answer he made to Melito.

were doing no harm. He doubts if a just emperor could have ordered anything so unjust ; and if the last order was really not from the emperor, the Christians entreat him not to give them up to their enemies.[4]   We conclude from this that there

4 Eusebius, IV. 26 ; and Routh's Reliquiae Sacrae, vol. I. and the notes. The interpretation of this Fragment is not easy. Mosheim misunderstood one passage so far as to affirm that Marcus promised rewards to those who denounced the Christians ; an interpretation which is entirely false. Melito calls the Christian religion "our philosophy," which began among barbarians (the Jews), and flourished among the Roman subjects in the time of Augustus, to the great advantage of the empire, for from that time the power of the Romans grew great and glorious. He says that the emperor has and will have as the successor to Augustus' power the good wishes of men, if he will protect that philosophy which grew up with the empire and began with Augustus, which philosophy the predecessors of Antoninus honored in addition to the other religions. He further says that the Christian religion had suffered no harm since the time of Augustus, but on the contrary had enjoyed all honor and respect that any man could desire. Nero and Domitian, he says, were alone persuaded by some malicious men to calumniate the Christian religion, and this was the origin of the false charges against the Christians. But this was corrected by the emperors who immediately preceded Antoninus, who often by their Rescripts reproved those who attempted to trouble the Christians. Hadrian, Antoninus' grandfather, wrote to many, and among them to the governor of Asia. Antoninus Pius when Marcus was associated with him in the empire wrote to the cities, that they must not trouble the Christians ; among others to the people of Larissa, Thessalonica, the Athenians and all the Greeks. Melito concluded thus : We are persuaded that thou who hast about these things the same mind that they had, nay rather one much more humane and philosophical, wilt do all that we ask thee. — This Apology was written after A. D. 16.), the year in which Verus died, for it speaks

were at least imperial Rescripts or Constitutions
of M. Antoninus, which were made the foundation of these persecutions. The fact of being a
Christian was now a crime and punished, unless
the accused denied their religion. Then come
the persecutions at Smyrna, which some modern
critics place in A. D. 167, ten years before the
persecution of Lyon. The governors of the provinces under M. Antoninus might have found
enough even in Trajan's Rescript to warrant them
in punishing Christians, and the fanaticism of the
people would drive them to persecution, even if
they were unwilling. But besides the fact of the
Christians rejecting all the heathen ceremonies,
we must not forget that they plainly maintained
that all the heathen religions were false. The
Christians thus declared war against the heathen
rites, and it is hardly necessary to observe that
this was a declaration of hostility against the
Roman government, which tolerated all the various forms of superstition that existed in the empire,
and could not consistently tolerate another religion,
which declared that all the rest were false, and all

of Marcus only and his son Commodus. According to
Melito's testimony, Christians had only been punished
for their religion in the time of Nero and Domitian, and
the persecutions began again in the time of M. Antoninus and were founded on his orders, which were abused
as he seems to mean. He distinctly affirms '' that the
race of the godly is now persecuted and harrassed by
fresh imperial orders in Asia, a thing which had never
happened before." But we know that all this is not
true, and that Christians had been punished in Trajan's
time.

the splendid ceremonies of the empire only a worship of devils.

If we had a true ecclesiastical history, we should know how the Roman emperors attempted to check the new religion, how they enforced their principle of finally punishing Christians, simply as Christians, which Justin in his Apology affirms that they did, and I have no doubt that he tells the truth; how far popular clamor and riots went in this matter, and how far many fanatical and ignorant Christians, for there were many such, contributed to excite the fanaticism on the other side and to embitter the quarrel between the Roman government and the new religion. Our extant ecclesiastical histories are manifestly falsified, and what truth they contain is grossly exaggerated; but the fact is certain that in the time of M. Antoninus the heathen populations were in open hostility to the Christians, and that under Antoninus' rule men were put to death because they were Christians. Eusebius in the preface to his fifth book remarks that in the seventeenth year of Antoninus' reign, in some parts of the world the persecution of the Christians became more violent, and that it proceeded from the populace in the cities; and he adds in his usual style of exaggeration, that we may infer from what took place in a single nation that myriads of martyrs were made in the habitable earth. The nation which he alludes to is Gallia; and he then proceeds to give the letter of the churches of Vienna and Lugdunum. It is probable that he has assigned the true cause of

the persecutions, the fanaticism of the populace,
and that both governors and emperor had a great
deal of trouble with these disturbances.   How
far Marcus was cognizant of these cruel proceed-
ings we do not know, for the historical records of
his reign are very defective.   He did not make
the rule against the Christians, for Trajan did
that ; and if we admit that he would have been
willing to let the Christians alone, we cannot
affirm that it was in his power, for it would be a
great mistake to suppose that Antoninus had the
unlimited authority, which some modern sovereigns
have had.   His power was limited by certain con-
stitutional forms, by the Senate, and by the prece-
dents of his predecessors.   We cannot admit that
such a man was an active persecutor, for there is
no evidence that he was, though it is certain that
he had no good opinion of the Christians, as appears from his own words.[5]   But he knew nothing

---

[5] See xi. 3.   The emperor probably speaks of such
fanatics as Clemens (quoted by Gataker on this passage)
mentions.   The rational Christians admitted no fellowship with them. "Some of these heretics," says Clemens,
" show their impiety and cowardice by loving their lives,
saying that the knowledge of the really existing God is
true testimony (martyrdom), but that a man is a self-
murderer who bears witness by his death. We also blame
those who rush to death, for there are some, not of us,
but only bearing the same name who give themselves
up.   We say of them that they die without being martyrs,
even if they are publicly punished ; and they give themselves up to a death which avails nothing, as the Indian
Gymnosophists give themselves up foolishly to fire."
Cave in his Primitive Christianity (ii. c. 7) says of the
Christians : "They did flock to the place of torment

of them except their hostility to the Roman religion, and he probably thought that they were
dangerous to the state, notwithstanding the pro-
fessions false or true of some of the Apologists.
So much I have said, because it would be unfair
not to state all that can be urged against a man
whom his contemporaries and subsequent ages
venerated as a model of virtue and benevolence.
If I admitted the genuineness of some documents,
he would be altogether clear from the charge of
even allowing any persecutions ; but as I seek the
truth and am sure that they are false, I leave him
to bear whatever blame is his due.   I add that it
is quite certain that Antoninus did not derive any
of his Ethical principles from a religion of which
he knew nothing.[6]

faster than droves of beasts that are driven to the sham-
bles.   They even longed to be in the arms of suffering.
Ignatius, though then in his journey to Rome in order
to his execution, yet by the way as he went could not
but vent his passionate desire of it: O that I might
come to those wild beasts, that are prepared for me ; I
heartily wish that I may presently meet with them ; I
would invite and encourage them speedily to devour me,
and not be afraid to set upon me as they have been to
others ; nay should they refuse it, I would even force
them to it ;" and more to the same purpose from Eusebius.
Cave, an honest and good man, says all this in praise of
the Christians ; but I think that he mistook the matter
We admire a man who holds to his principles even to
death ; but these fanatical Christians are the Gymnosophists whom Clemens treats with disdain.

   [6] Dr F. C. Baur in his work entitled Das Christenthum
und die Christliche Kirche der drei ersten Jahrhunderte,
&c. has examined this question with great good sense
and fairness, and I believe he has stated the truth as near
as our authorities enable us to reach it.

There is no doubt that the Emperor's Reflec‹
tions or his Meditations, as they are generally
named, is a genuine work. In the first book he
speaks of himself, his family, and his teachers ;
and in other books he mentions himself. Suidas
(v. Μάρκος) notices a work of Antoninus in twelve
books, which he names the " conduct of his own
life ; " and he cites the book under several words
in his Dictionary, giving the emperor's name, but
not the title of the work. There are also passages
cited by Suidas from Antoninus without mention
of the emperor's name. The true title of the
work is unknown. Xylander who published the
first edition of this book (Zürich, 1558, 8vo., with a
Latin version) used a manuscript, which contained
the twelve books, but it is not known where the
manuscript is now. The only other complete
manuscript which is known to exist is in the Vatican library, but it has no title and no inscriptions
of the several books : the eleventh only has the
inscription Μάρκου αὐτοκράτορος marked with an
asterisk. The other Vatican manuscripts and the
three Florentine contain only excerpts from the
emperor's book. All the titles of the excerpts
nearly agree with that which Xylander prefixed
to his edition, Μάρκου ᾿Αντωνίνου Αὐτοκράτορος τῶν
εἰς ἑαυτὸν βιβλία ιβ. This title has been used by
all subsequent editors. We cannot tell whether
Antoninus divided his work into books or some-
body else did it. If the inscriptions at the end of
the first and second books are genuine, he may
have made the division himself.

It is plain that the emperor wrote down his
thoughts or reflections as the occasions arose ; and
since they were intended for his own use, it is no
improbable conjecture that he left a complete copy
behind him written with his own hand ; for it is
not likely that so diligent a man would use the
labor of a transcriber for such a purpose, and
expose his most secret thoughts to any other eye.
He may have also intended the book for his son
Commodus, who however had no taste for his
father's philosophy. Some careful hand preserved
the precious volume ; and a work by Antoninus
is mentioned by other late writers besides Suidas.

Many critics have labored on the text of Antoninus. The most complete edition is that by
Thomas Gataker, 1652, 4to. The second edition
of Gataker was superintended by George Stan-
hope, 1697, 4to. There is also an edition of 1704.
Gataker made and suggested many good corrections, and he also made a new Latin version, which
is not a very good specimen of Latin, but it
generally expresses the sense of the original and
often better than some of the more recent translations. He added in the margin opposite to each
paragraph references to the other parallel passages ;
and he wrote a commentary, one of the most complete that has been written on any ancient author.
This commentary contains the editor's exposition
of the more difficult passages, and quotations from
all the Greek and Roman writers for the illustra-
tion of the text. It is a wonderful monument of
learning and labor, and certainly no Englishman

has yet done anything like it. At the end of his preface the editor says that he wrote it at Rotherhithe near London in a severe winter, when he was in the seventy-eighth year of his age, 1651, a time when Milton, Selden and other great men of the Commonwealth time were living ; and the great French scholar Saumaise (Salmasius), with whom Gataker corresponded and received help from him for his edition of Antoninus. The Greek text has also been edited by J. M. Schultz, Leipzig, 1802. 8vo. ; and by the learned Greek Adamantius Coraïs, Paris, 1816, 8vo. The text of Schultz was republished by Tauchnitz, 1821.

There are English, French, Italian and Spanish translations of M. Antoninus, and there may be others. I have not seen all the English translations. There is one by Jeremy Collier, 1702, 8vo. a most coarse and vulgar copy of the original. The latest French translation by Alexis Pierron in the collection of Charpentier is better than Dacier's, which has been honored with an Italian version (Udine, 1772). There is an Italian version (1675) which I have not seen. It is by a cardinal. " A man illustrious in the church, the Cardinal Francis Barberini the elder, nephew of Pope Urban VIII, occupied the last years of his life in translating into his native language the thoughts of the Roman emperor, in order to diffuse among the faithful the fertilizing and vivifying seeds. He dedicated this translation to his soul, to make it, as he says in his energetic style, redder than his purple at the sight of the virtues

of this Gentile " (Pierron. Preface). I have made
this translation at intervals after having used the
book for many years. It is made from the Greek,
but I have not always followed one text. I have
occasionally compared other versions. I made
this translation for my own use, because I found
that it was worth the labor. It may be useful
to others also and at last I have determined to
print it, though, as the original is both very difficult
to understand and still more difficult to translate,
it is not possible that I have always avoided error.
But I believe that I have not often missed the
meaning, and those who will take the trouble to
compare the translation with the original should
not hastily conclude that I am wrong, if they do
not agree with me. Some passages do give the
meaning, though at first sight they may not appear
to do so ; and when I differ from the translators,
I think that in some places they are wrong, and in
other places I am sure that they are. I have
placed a † in some passages, which indicates corruption in the text or great uncertainty in the
meaning. I could have made the language more
easy and flowing, but I have preferred a somewhat
ruder style as being better suited to express the
character of the original ; and sometimes the obscurity which may appear in the version is a fair
copy of the obscurity of the Greek. If I should
ever revise this version, I would gladly make use
of any corrections which may be suggested. I
have added an index of some of the Greek terms
with the corresponding English. If I have not

given the best words for the Greek, I have done the best that I could ; and in the text I have always given the same translation of the same word.

The last reflection of the Stoic philosophy that I have observed is in Simplicius' Commentary on the Enchiridion of Epictetus. Simplicius was not a Christian, and such a man was not likely to be converted at a time when Christianity was grossly corrupted. But he was a really religious man, and he concludes his commentary with a prayer to the Deity which no Christian could improve. From the time of Zeno to Simplicius, a period of about nine hundred years, the Stoic philosophy formed the characters of some of the best and greatest men. Finally it became extinct, and we hear no more of it till the revival of letters in Italy. Angelo Poliziano met with two very inaccurate and incomplete manuscripts of Epictetus' Enchiridion, which he translated into Latin and dedicated to his great patron Lorenzo de' Medici in whose collection he had found the book. Poliziano's version was printed in the first Bâle edition of the Enchiridion, A. D. 1531 (apud And. Cratandrum). Poliziano recommends the Enchiridion to Lorenzo as a work well suited to his temper, and useful in the difficulties by which he was surrounded.

Epictetus and Antoninus have had readers ever since they were first printed. The little book of Antoninus has been the companion of some great men. Machiavelli's Art of War and Marcus Antoninus were the two books which were used

when he was a young man by Captain John
Smith, and he could not have found two writers
better fitted to form the character of a soldier
and a man.   Smith is almost unknown and forgotten in England his native country, but not in
America where he saved the young colony of Vir-
ginia.   He was great in his heroic mind and his
deeds in arms, but greater still in the nobleness of
his character.   For a man's greatness lies not in
wealth and station, as the vulgar believe, nor yet
in his intellectual capacity, which is often associated with the meanest moral character, the most
abject servility to those in high places and arrogance to the poor and lowly ; but a man's true
greatness lies in the consciousness of an honest
purpose in life, founded on a just estimate of himself and everything else, on frequent self-exami-
nation, and a steady obedience to the rule which
he knows to be right, without troubling himself,
as the emperor says he should not, about what
others may think or say, or whether they do or do
not do that which he thinks and says and does.

PHILOSOPHY OF ANTONINUS.

T has been said that the Stoic philosophy first showed its real value
when it passed from Greece to Rome.
The doctrines of Zeno and his suc-
cessors were well suited to the gravity and practical good sense of the Romans; and even in the
Republican period we have an example of a man,
M. Cato Uticensis, who lived the life of a Stoic
and died consistently with the opinions which he
professed. He was a man, says Cicero, who em-
braced the Stoic philosophy from conviction; not
for the purpose of vain discussion, as most did, but
in order to make his life conformable to its precepts. In the wretched times from the death of
Augustus to the murder of Domitian, there was
nothing but the Stoic philosophy which could con-
sole and support the followers of the old religion
under imperial tyranny and amidst universal corruption. There were even then noble minds that
could dare and endure, sustained by a good conscience and an elevated idea of the purposes of
man's existence. Such were Paetus Thrasea,

Helvidius Priscus, Cornutus, C. Musonius Rufus,[1] and the poets Persius and Juvenal, whose energetic language and manly thoughts may be as instructive to us now as they might have been to their contemporaries. Persius died under Nero's bloody reign, but Juvenal had the good fortune to survive the tyrant Domitian and to see the better times of Nerva, Trajan and Hadrian. His best precepts are derived from the Stoic school, and they are enforced in his finest verses by the unrivalled vigor of the Latin language.

The two best expounders of the later Stoical philosophy were a Greek slave and a Roman emperor. Epictetus, a Phrygian Greek, was brought to Rome, we know not how, but he was there the slave and afterwards the freedman of an unworthy master, Epaphroditus by name, himself a freedman and a favorite of Nero. Epictetus may have been a hearer of C. Musonius Rufus, while he was still a slave, but he can hardly have been a teacher before he was made free. He was one of the philosophers whom Domitian's order banished from Rome. He retired to Nicopolis in Epirus, and he may have died there. Like other great teachers he wrote nothing, and we are indebted to his grateful pupil Arrian for what we have of

---

[1] I have omitted Seneca, Nero's preceptor. He was in a sense a Stoic and he has said many good things in a very fine way. There is a judgment of Gellius (XII. 2) on Seneca, or rather a statement of what some people thought of his philosophy, and it is not favorable. His writings and his life must be taken together, and I have nothing more to say of him here.

Epictetus' discourses. Arrian wrote eight books
of the discourses of Epictetus, of which only four
remain and some fragments. We have also from
Arrian's hand the small Enchiridion or Manual
of the chief precepts of Epictetus. There is a
valuable commentary on the Enchiridion by Simplicius, who lived in the time of the emperor Jus-
tinian.[2]

Antoninus in his first book (I. 7), in which he
gratefully commemorates his obligations to his
teachers, says that he was made acquainted by
Junius Rusticus with the discourses of Epictetus,
whom he mentions also in other passages (IV. 41;
XI. 33. 36). Indeed, the doctrines of Epictetus
and Antoninus are the same, and Epictetus is the
best authority for the explanation of the philosophical language of Antoninus and the exposition of his opinions. But the method of the
two philosophers is entirely different. Epictetus
addressed himself to his hearers in a continuous
discourse and in a familiar and simple manner.
Antoninus wrote down his reflections for his own
use only, in short unconnected paragraphs, which
are often obscure.

The Stoics made three divisions of philosophy,
Physic (φυσικόν), Ethic (ἠθικόν), and Logic (λογι-
κόν). This division, we are told by Diogenes, was
made by Zeno of Citium, the founder of the Stoic

_____

[2] There is a complete edition of Arrian's Epictetus
with the commentary of Simplicius by J. Schweighaeu-
ser, 6 vols. 8vo. 1799, 1800. There is also an English
translation of Epictetus by Mrs. Carter.

sect and by Chrysippus ; but these philosophers placed the three divisions in the following order, Logic, Physic, Ethic. It appears however that this division was made before Zeno's time and acknowledged by Plato, as Cicero remarks (Acad. Post. i. 5). Logic is not synonymous with our term Logic in the narrower sense of that word.

Cleanthes, a Stoic, subdivided the three divisions, and made six : Dialectic and Rhetoric, comprised in Logic ; Ethic and Politic ; Physic and Theology. This division was merely for practical use, for all Philosophy is one. Even among the earliest Stoics Logic or Dialectic does not occupy the same place as in Plato : it is considered only as an instrument which is to be used for the other divisions of Philosophy. An exposition of the earlier Stoic doctrines and of their modifications would require a volume. My object is to explain only the opinions of Antoninus, so far as they can be collected from his book.

According to the subdivision of Cleanthes, Physic and Theology go together, or the study of the nature of Things, and the study of the nature of the Deity, so far as man can understand the Deity, and of his government of the universe. This division or subdivision is not formally adopted by Antoninus, for as already observed, there is no method in his book ; but it is virtually contained in it.

Cleanthes also connects Ethic and Politic, or the study of the principles of morals and the study of the constitution of civil society ; and undoubt-

edly he did well in subdividing Ethic into two
parts, Ethic in the narrower sense and Politic, for
though the two are intimately connected, they are
also very distinct, and many questions can only be
properly discussed by carefully observing the distinction.   Antoninus does not treat of Politic.
His subject is Ethic, and Ethic in its practical
application to his own conduct in life as a man
and as a governor.   His Ethic is founded on his
doctrines about man's nature, the Universal Nature, and the relation of every man to everything
else.   It is therefore intimately and inseparably
connected with Physic or the nature of Things
and with Theology or the nature of the Deity.
He advises us to examine well all the impressions on our minds (φαντασία·) and to form a
right judgment of them, to make just conclusions,
and to inquire into the meanings of words, and
so far to apply Dialectic, but he has no attempt
at any exposition of Dialectic, and his philosophy
is in substance purely moral and practical.   He
says (VIII. 13), " Constantly and, if it be possible,
on the occasion of every impression on the soul,[3]

---

[3] The original is ἐπὶ πάσης φαντασίας. We have no
word which expresses φαντασία, for it is not only the sensuous appearance which comes from an external object,
which object is called τὸ φανταστόν, but it is also the
thought or feeling or opinion which is produced even
when there is no corresponding external object before us.
Accordingly everything which moves the soul is φανταστόν and produces a φαντασία.

   In this extract Antoninus says φυσιολογεῖν, παθολογεῖν,
διαλεκτικεύεσθαι.   I have translated παθολογεῖν by using
the word Moral (Ethic), and that is the meaning here.

apply to it the principles of Physic, of Moral and
of Dialectic : " which is only another way of tell-
ing us to examine the impression in every possible way. In another passage (III. 11) he says,
" To the aids which have been mentioned let this
one still be added : make for thyself a definition
or description of the object (τὸ φαιτασ́τόν) which
is presented to thee, so as to see distinctly what
kind of a thing it is in its substance, in its nudity,
in its complete entirety, and tell thyself its proper
name, and the names of the things of which it
has been compounded, and into which it will be
resolved." Such an examination implies a use
of Dialectic, which Antoninus accordingly employed as a means towards establishing his Physical, Theological and Ethical principles.

There are several expositions of the Physical,
Theological, and Ethical principles, which are
contained in the work of Antoninus ; and more
expositions than I have read. Ritter (Geschichte
der Philosophie, IV. 241) after explaining the
doctrines of Epictetus, treats very briefly and in-
sufficiently those of Antoninus. But he refers to
a short essay, in which the work is done better.[4]
There is also an essay on the Philosophical Principles of M. Aurelius Antoninus by J. M. Schultz,
placed at the end of his German translation of
Antoninus (Schleswig, 1799). With the assistance
of these two useful essays and his own diligent

---

4 De Marco Aurelio Antonino ... ex ipsius Commen-
tariis. Scriptio Philologica. Instituit Nicolaus Bachius,
Lipsiae, 1826.

study a man may form a sufficient notion of the
principles of Antoninus; but he will find it more
difficult to expound them to others. Besides the
want of arrangement in the original and of connection among the numerous paragraphs, the corruption of the text, the obscurity of the language
and the style, and sometimes perhaps the confusion in the writer's own ideas, — besides all this
there is occasionally an apparent contradiction in
the emperor's thoughts, as if his principles were
sometimes unsettled, as if doubt sometimes
clouded his mind.   A man who leads a life of
tranquillity and reflection, who is not disturbed
at home and meddles not with the affairs of the
world, may keep his mind at ease and his thoughts
in one even course.   But such a man has not
been tried.   All his Ethical philosophy and his
passive virtue might turn out to be idle words, if
he were once exposed to the rude realities of human existence.   Fine thoughts and moral disser-
tations from men who have not worked and suffered may be read, but they will be forgotten.
No religion, no Ethical philosophy is worth anything, if the teacher has not lived the " life of an
apostle," and been ready to die " the death of a
martyr."   " Not in passivity (the passive affects)
but in activity lie the evil and the good of the
rational social animal, just as his virtue and his
vice lie not in passivity, but in activity " (IX. 16).
The emperor Antoninus was a practical moralist.
From his youth he followed a laborious discipline,
and though his high station placed him above all

want or the fear of it, he lived as frugally and
temperately as the poorest philosopher. Epictetus
wanted little, and it seems that he always had
the little that he wanted ; and he was content with
it, as he had been with his servile station. But
Antoninus after his accession to the empire sat on
an uneasy seat. He had the administration of an
empire which extended from the Euphrates to the
Atlantic, from the cold mountains of Scotland to
the hot sands of Africa ; and we may imagine,
though we cannot know it by experience, what
must be the trials, the troubles, the anxiety and
the sorrows of him who has the world's business
on his hands with the wish to do the best that he
can, and the certain knowledge that he can do
very little of the good which he wishes.

In the midst of war, pestilence, conspiracy, general corruption and with the weight of so un-
wieldy an empire upon him, we may easily comprehend that Antoninus often had need of all his
fortitude to support him. The best and the bravest
men have moments of doubt and of weakness, but
if they are the best and the bravest, they rise again
from their depression by recurring to first principles,
as Antoninus does. The emperor says that life
is smoke, a vapor, and St. James in his Epistle
is of the same mind ; that the world is full of envious, jealous, malignant people, and a man might
be well content to get out of it. He has doubts
perhaps sometimes even about that to which he
holds most firmly. There are only a few passages
of this kind, but they are evidence of the struggles

which even the noblest of the sons of men had to maintain against the hard realities of his daily life. A poor remark it is which I have seen somewhere, and made in a disparaging way, that the emperor's reflections show that he had need of consolation and comfort in life, and even to prepare him to meet his death. True that he did need comfort and support, and we see how he found it. He constantly recurs to his fundamental principle that the universe is wisely ordered, that every man is a part of it and must conform to that order which he cannot change, that whatever the Deity has done is good, that all mankind are a man's brethren, that he must love and cherish them and try to make them better, even those who would do him harm. This is his conclusion (II. 17): " What then is that which is able to conduct a man? One thing and only one, Philosophy. But this consists in keeping the divinity within a man free from violence and unharmed, superior to pains and pleasures, doing nothing without a purpose nor yet falsely and with hypocrisy, not feeling the need of another man's doing or not doing anything; and besides, accepting all that happens and all that is allotted, as coming from thence, wherever it is, from whence he himself came; and finally waiting for death with a cheerful mind as being nothing else than a dissolution of the elements, of which every living being is compounded. But if there is no harm to the elements themselves in each continually changing into another, why should a man have any apprehension about the change and dissolution of all the elements [himself]? for it is according to nature; and nothing is evil that is according to nature."

The Physic of Antoninus is the knowledge of the Nature of the Universe, of its government, and of the relation of man's nature to both. He names the universe (ἡ τῶν ὅλων οὐσία. VI. 1),[5] "the universal substance," and he adds that "reason," (λόγος) governs the universe. He also (VI. 9) uses the terms "universal nature" or "nature of the universe." He (VI. 25) calls the universe "the one and all, which we name Cosmus or Order" (κόσμος). If he ever seems to use these general terms as significant of the All, of all that man can in any way conceive to exist, he still on other occasions plainly distinguishes between Matter, Material things (ὕλη, ὑλικόν), and Cause, Origin,

---

[5] As to the word οὐσία, the reader may see the Index. I add here a few examples of the use of the word; Antoninus has (V. 24), ἡ συμπᾶσα οὐσία. "the universal substance." He says (XII. 30), "there is one common" substance (οὐσία), distributed among countless bodies; and (IV. 40). In Stobaeus (tom. I. lib. 1, tit. 14) there is this definition, οὐσίαν δέ φασιν τῶν ὄντων ἁπάντων τὴν πρώτην ὕλην. (In VIII. 11), Antoninus speaks of τὸ οὐσιῶδες καὶ ὑλικόν, "the substantial and the material;" and (VII. 10) he says that "everything material" (ἔνυλον) disappears in the substance of the whole (τῇ τῶν ὅλων οὐσίᾳ). The οὐσία is the generic name of that existence, which we assume as the highest or ultimate, because we conceive no existence which can be coördinated with it and none above it. It is the philosopher's "substance:" it is the ultimate expression for that which we conceive or suppose to be the basis, the being of a thing. "From the Divine, which is substance in itself, or the only and sole substance, all and everything that is created exists." (Swedenborg)

Reason (αἰτία, αἰτιῶδες, λόγος).[6]   This is conformable to Zeno's doctrine that there are two original
principles (ἀρχαί) of all things, that which acts
(τὸ ποιοῦν) and that which is acted upon (τὸ
πάσχον).   That which is acted on is the formless
matter (ὕλη) : that which acts is the reason (λόγος)
in it, God, for he is eternal and operates through
all matter, and produces all things.   So Antoninus (v. 32) speaks of the reason (λόγος) which
pervades all substance (οὐσία), and through all
time by fixed periods (revolutions) administers
the universe (τὸ πᾶν).   God is eternal, and Matter is eternal.   It is God who gives to matter its

---

[6] I remark, in order to anticipate any misapprehension,
that all these general terms involve a contradiction. The
"one and all," and the like, and "the whole," imply
limitation. "One" is limited; "all" is limited; the
"whole" is limited. We cannot help it. We cannot find
words to express that which we cannot fully conceive.
The addition of "absolute" or any other such word does
not mend the matter. Even God is used by most people,
often unconsciously, in such a way that limitation is implied, and yet at the same time words are added which are
intended to deny limitation. A Christian martyr, when
he was asked what God was, is said to have answered that
God has no name like a man ; and Justin says the same
(Apol. II. 6). We can conceive the existence of a thing,
or rather we may have the idea of an existence, without
an adequate notion of it, "adequate" meaning coexten-
sive and coequal with the thing.   We have a notion of
limited space derived from the dimensions of what we
call a material thing, though of space absolute, if I may
use the term, we have no notion at all ; and of infinite
space the notion is the same, no notion at all ; and yet
we conceive it in a sense, though I know not how, and
we believe that space is infinite, and we cannot conceive
it to be finite.

form, but he is not said to have created matter.
According to this view, which is as old as Anaxagoras, God and matter exist independently, but
God governs matter.   This doctrine is simply the
expression of the fact of the existence both of
matter and of God.   The Stoics did not perplex
themselves with the insoluble question of the origin
and nature of matter.[7]   Antoninus also assumes a
beginning of things, as we now know them ; but
his language is sometimes very obscure.   I have
endeavored to explain the meaning of one difficult
passage. (VII. 75, and the note.)

Matter consists of elemental parts ($\sigma\tau o\iota\chi\epsilon\tilde{\iota}a$)
of which all material objects are made.   But
nothing is permanent in form.   The nature of
the universe, according to Antoninus' expression
(IV. 36), "loves nothing so much as to change
the things which are, and to make new things
like them.   For everything that exists is in a
manner the seed of that which will be.   But thou
art thinking only of seeds which are cast into the

---

[7] The notions of matter and of space are inseparable.
We derive the notion of space from matter and form. But
we have no adequate conception either of matter or of
space. Matter in its ultimate resolution is as unintelligible
as what men call mind, spirit, or by whatever other name
they may express the power which makes itself known by
its acts. Anaxagoras laid down the distinction between
intelligence ($\nu o\tilde{\nu}\varsigma$) and matter, and he said that intelligence impressed motion on matter and so separated the
elements of matter and gave them order ; but he probably
only assumed a beginning, as Simplicius says, as a
foundation of his philosophical teaching.

The common Greek word which we translate "**matter**"
is $\tilde{\nu}\lambda\eta$.   It is the stuff that things are made of.

earth or into a womb: but this is a very vulgar notion." All things then are in a constant flux and change : some things are dissolved into the elements, others come in their places ; and so the " whole universe continues ever young and perfect." (XII. 23.)

Antoninus has some obscure expressions about what he calls " seminal principles " (σπερματικοὶ λόγοι). He opposes them to the Epicurean atoms (VI. 24), and consequently his "seminal principles" are not material atoms which wander about at hazard, and combine nobody knows how. In one passage (IV. 21) he speaks of living principles, souls (ψυχαὶ) after the dissolution of their bodies being received into the " seminal principle of the universe." Schultz thinks that by " seminal principles Antoninus means the relations of the various elemental principles, which relations are determined by the Deity and by which alone the production of organized beings is possible." This may be the meaning, but if it is, nothing of any value can be derived from it.[8] Antoninus often uses the word " Nature " (φύσις), and we must attempt to fix its meaning. The simple etymological sense of φύσις is " production," the birth of

---

[8] Justin (Apol. II. 8) has the expression κατὰ σπερματικοῦ λόγου μέρος, where he is speaking of the Stoics. The early Christian writers were familiar with the Stoic terms, and their writings show that the contest was begun between the Christian expositors and the Greek philosophy. Even in the second Epistle of St. Peter (II. 1, v. 4) we find a Stoic expression, ἵνα διὰ τούτων γένησθε θείας κοινωνοὶ φύσεως.

what we call Things. The Romans used Natura,
which also means "birth" originally. But neither
the Greeks nor the Romans stuck to this simple
meaning, nor do we. Antoninus says (x. 6):
" Whether the universe is [a concourse of] atoms
or Nature [is a system], let this first be established that I am a part of the whole which is
governed by nature." Here it might seem as if
nature were personified and viewed as an active,
efficient power, as something which, if not independent of the Deity, acts by a power which is
given to it by the Deity. Such, if I understand
the expression right, is the way in which the word
Nature is often used now, though it is plain that
many writers use the word without fixing any
exatc meaning to it. It is the same with the
expression Laws of Nature, which some writers
may use in an intelligible sense, but others as
clearly use in no definite sense at all. There is
no meaning in this word Nature, except that which
Bishop Butler assigns to it, when he says, " The
only distinct meaning of that word Natural is
Stated, Fixed or Settled; since what is natural as
much requires and presupposes an intelligent agent
to render it so, i. e. to effect it continually or at
stated times, as what is supernatural or miraculous
does to effect it at once." This is Plato's meaning
(De Leg. IV.), when he says, that God holds the
beginning and end and middle of all that exists,
and proceeds straight on his course, making his
circuit according to nature (that is, by a fixed
order); and he is continually accompanied by jus-

4

tice who punishes those who deviate from the divine law, that is, from the order or course which God observes.

When we look at the motions of the planets, the action of what we call gravitation, the elemental combination of unorganized bodies and their reso- lution, the production of plants and of living bodies, their generation, growth, and their disso- lution, which we call their death, we observe a regular sequence of phaenomena, which within the limits of experience present and past, so far as we know the past, is fixed and invariable. But if this is not so, if the order and sequence of phae- nomena, as known to us, are subject to change in the course of an infinite progression, — and such change is conceivable, — we have not discovered, nor shall we ever discover, the whole of the order and sequence of phaenomena, in which sequence there may be involved according to its very nature, that is, according to its fixed order, some varia- tion of what we now call the Order or Nature of Things. It is also conceivable that such changes have taken place, changes in the order of things, as we are compelled by the imperfection of lan- guage to call them, but which are no changes ; and further it is certain, that our knowledge of the true sequence of all actual phaenomena, as for instance, the phaenomena of generation, growth, and dissolution, is and ever must be imperfect.

We do not fare much better when we speak of Causes and Effects than when we speak of Nature. For the practical purposes of life we may use the

terms cause and effect conveniently, and we may
fix a distinct meaning to them, distinct enough at
least to prevent all misunderstanding. But the
case is different when we speak of causes and
effects as of Things. All that we know is phaenomena, as the Greeks called them, or appearances
which follow one another in a regular order, as
we conceive it, so that if some one phaenomenon
should fail in the series, we conceive that there
must either be an interruption of the series, or
that something else will appear after the phaenomenon which has failed to appear, and will
occupy the vacant place ; and so the series in its
progression may be modified or totally changed.
Cause and effect then mean nothing in the sequence of natural phaenomena beyond what I have
said ; and the real cause, or the transcendent cause,
as some would call it, of each successive phaenomenon is in that which is the cause of all things
which are, which have been, and which will be
forever. Thus the word Creation may have a
real sense if we consider it as the first, if we can
conceive a first, in the present order of natural
phaenomena ; but in the vulgar sense a creation
of all things at a certain time, followed by a
quiescence of the first cause and an abandonment
of all sequences of Phaenomena to the Laws of
Nature, or to any other words that people may
use, is absolutely absurd. [9]

[9] Time and space are the conditions of our thought;
but time infinite and space infinite cannot be objects of
thought, except in a very imperfect way. Time and space

Now, though there is great difficulty in understanding all the passages of Antoninus, in which
he speaks of Nature, of the changes of things and
of the economy of the universe, I am convinced
that his sense of Nature and Natural is the same
as that which I have stated ; and as he was a man
who knew how to use words in a clear way and
with strict consistency, we ought to assume, even
if his meaning in some passages is doubtful, that
his view of Nature was in harmony with his fixed
belief in the all-pervading, ever-present, and ever-
active energy of God. (iv. 40 ; x. 1 ; vi. 40 ; and
other passages.)

There is much in Antoninus that is hard to
understand, and it might be said that he did not
fully comprehend all that he wrote ; which would
however be in no way remarkable, for it happens
now that a man may write what neither he nor
anybody can understand.   Antoninus tells us
(xii. 10) to look at things and see what they are,
resolving them into the material ($\ddot{v}\lambda\eta$), the causal
($a\ddot{i}\tau\iota o\nu$), and the relation ($\dot{a}\nu a\phi o\rho\dot{a}$), or the purpose, by which he seems to mean something in the

must not in any way be thought of, when we think of the
Deity. Swedenborg says, " The natural man may believe
that he would have no thought, if the ideas of time, of
space, and of things material were taken away ; for upon
those is founded all the thought that man has.   But let
him know that the thoughts are limited and confined in
proportion as they partake of time, of space, and of what
is material ; and that they are not limited and are extended, in proportion as they do not partake of those things ;
since the mind is so far elevated above the things corporeal and worldly." (Concerning Heaven and Hell, 169.)

nature of what we call effect, or end. The word
cause (αἰτία) is the difficulty. There is the same
word in the Sanscrit (*hétu*); and the subtle philosophers of India and of Greece, and the less
subtle philosophers of modern times have all used
this word, or an equivalent word, in a vague way.
Yet the confusion sometimes may be in the in-
evitable ambiguity of language rather than in the
mind of the writer, for I cannot think that some
of the wisest of men did not know what they intended to say. When Antoninus says (IV. 36),
" that everything that exists is in a manner the
seed of that which will be," he might be supposed
to say what some of the Indian philosophers have
said, and thus a profound truth might be converted
into a gross absurdity. But he says, " in a manner," and in a manner he said true ; and in
another manner, if you mistake his meaning, he
said false. When Plato said, " Nothing ever is,
but is always becoming " (ἀεὶ γίγνεται), he delivered a text, out of which we may derive something ; for he destroys by it not all practical, but
all speculative notions of cause and effect. The
whole series of things, as they appear to us, must
be contemplated in time, that is in succession, and
we conceive or suppose intervals between one state
of things and another state of things, so that there
is priority and sequence, and interval, and Being,
and a ceasing to Be, and beginning and ending.
But there is nothing of the kind in the Nature of
Things. It is an everlasting continuity. (IV. 45 ;
VII. 75.) When Antoninus speaks of generation

(x. 26), he speaks of one cause (αἰτία) acting,
and then another cause taking up the work, which
the former left in a certain state, and so on ; and
we might perhaps conceive that he had some notion like what has been called " the self-evolving
power of nature ; " a fine phrase indeed, the full
import of which I believe that the writer of it
did not see, and thus he laid himself open to the
imputation of being a follower of one of the
Hindu sects, which makes all things come by
evolution out of nature or matter, or out of something which takes the place of deity, but is not
deity. I would have all men think as they please
or as they can, and I only claim the same freedom, which I give.   When a man writes anything, we may fairly try to find out all that his
words must mean, even if the result is that they
mean what he did not mean ; and if we find this
contradiction, it is not our fault, but his misfortune.   Now Antoninus is perhaps somewhat in
this condition in what he says (x. 26), though he
speaks at the end of the paragraph of the power
which acts, unseen by the eyes, but still no less
clearly.   But whether in this passage (x. 26) he
means that the power is conceived to be in the
different successive causes (αἰτίαι), or in something else, nobody can tell.   From other passages
however I do collect that his notion of the phaenomena of the universe is what I have stated.
The deity works unseen, if we may use such language, and perhaps I may, as Job did, or he who
wrote the book of Job.   " In him we live and

move and are," said St. Paul to the Athenians,
and to show his hearers that this was no new
doctrine, he quoted the Greek poets.   One of
these poets was the Stoic Cleanthes whose noble
hymn to Zeus or God is an elevated expression
of devotion and philosophy.   It deprives Nature
of her power and puts her under the immediate
government of the deity.

" Thee all this heaven, which whirls around the earth,
   Obeys and willing follows where thou leadest. —
   Without thee, God, nothing is done on earth,
   Nor in the æthereal realms, nor in the sea,
   Save what the wicked do through their own folly."

Antoninus' conviction of the existence of a
divine power and government was founded on his
perception of the order of the universe.   Like
Socrates (Xen. Mem. iv. 3), he says that though
we cannot see the forms of divine powers, we
know that they exist because we see their works.
   " To those who ask, Where hast thou seen the
gods, or how dost thou comprehend that they exist and so worshipest them ? I answer, in the first
place, that they may be seen even with the eyes;
in the second place, neither have I seen my own
soul and yet I honor it.   Thus then with respect
to the gods, from what I constantly experience of
their power, from this I comprehend that they
exist and I venerate them."   (xii. 28. Comp.
Xen. Mem. i. 4, 9 ; St. Paul's Epistle to the Romans, i. 19, 20 ; and Montaigne's Apology for
Raimond de Sebonde, ii. c. 12.)   This is a very
old argument which has always had great weight

with most people and has appeared sufficient. It
does not acquire the least additional strength by
being developed in a learned treatise. It is as
intelligible in its simple enunciation as it can be
made. If it is rejected, there is no arguing with
him who rejects it : and if it is worked out into
innumerable particulars, the value of the evidence runs the risk of being buried under a mass
of words.

Man being conscious that he is a spiritual power
or an intellectual power, or that he has such a
power, in whatever way he conceives that he has
it — for I wish simply to state a fact — from this
power which he has in himself, he is led, as Antoninus says, to believe that there is a greater
power, which as the old Stoics tell us, pervades
the whole universe as the intellect [10] (νοῦς) per-

[10] I have always translated the word νοῦς, "intelligence " or "intellect." It appears to be the word used by
the oldest Greek philosophers to express the notion of
" intelligence " as opposed to the notion of " matter." I
have always translated the word λόγος by "reason," and
λογικός by the word "rational," or perhaps sometimes
"reasonable," as I have translated νοερός by the word
"intellectual." Every man who has thought and has
read any philosophical writings knows the difficulty of
finding words to express certain notions, how imperfectly
words express these notions, and how carelessly the words
are often used. The various senses of the word λόγος are
enough to perplex any man. Our translators of the New
Testament (St. John, c. i.) have simply translated ὁ λόγος
by "the word," as the Germans translated it by "das
Wort ;" but in their theological writings they sometimes
retain the original term Logos. The Germans have a
term Vernunft, which seems to come nearest to our word
Reason, or the necessary and absolute truths which we

vades man. (Compare Epictetus' Discourses, I.
14; and Voltaire à Made. Necker, vol. LXVII. p.
278.)

God exists then, but what do we know of his
Nature? Antoninus says that the soul of man is
an efflux from the divinity. We have bodies
like animals, but we have reason, intelligence as
the gods. Animals have life (ψυχή), and what
we call instincts or natural principles of action :
but the rational animal man alone has a rational,
intelligent soul (ψυχὴ λογικ́η, νοερά). Antoninus
insists on this continually : God is in man,[11] and
so we must constantly attend to the divinity
within us, for it is only in this way that we can
have any knowledge of the nature of God. The
human soul is in a sense a portion of the divinity,
and the soul alone has any communication with

cannot conceive as being other than what they are. Such
are what some people have called the laws of thought,
the conceptions of space and of time, and axioms or first
principles, which need no proof and cannot be proved or
denied. Accordingly the Germans can say " Gott ist die
höchste Vernunft," the Supreme Reason. The Germans
have also a word Verstand, which seems to represent our
word " understanding," " intelligence," " intellect," not
as a thing absolute which exists by itself, but as a thing
connected with an individual being, as a man. Accordingly it is the capacity of receiving impressions (Vorstel-
lungen, φαντασίαι), and forming from them distinct ideas,
(Begriffe), and perceiving differences. I do not think
that these remarks will help the reader to the understanding of Antoninus, or his use of the words νοῦς and λόγος.
The Emperor's meaning must be got from his own words,
and if it does not agree altogether with modern notions,
it is not our business to force it into agreement, but simply to find out what his meaning is, if we can.

[11] Comp. Ep. to the Corinthians, I. 3. 17.

the Deity, for as he says (XII. 2) : " With his
intellectual part alone God touches the intelligence only which has flowed and been derived
from himself into these bodies." In fact he says
that which is hidden within a man is life, that is
the man himself. All the rest is vesture, covering, organs, instrument, which the living man, the
real [12] man, uses for the purposes of his present
existence. The air is universally diffused for him
who is able to respire, and so for him who is will-

[12] This is also Swedenborg's doctrine of the soul. "As
to what concerns the soul, of which it is said that it shall
live after death, it is nothing else but the man himself,
who lives in the body, that is, the interior man, who by
the body acts in the world and from whom the body itself
lives " (quoted by Clissold, p. 456 of " The Practical Nature of the Theological Writings of Emanuel Swedenborg,
in a letter to the Archbishop of Dublin." second edition,
1859 ; a book which theologians might read with profit).
This is an old doctrine of the soul, which has been often
proclaimed, but never better expressed than by the
" Auctor de Mundo," c. 6, quoted by Gataker in his
" Antoninus," p. 436. " The soul by which we live and
have cities and houses is invisible, but it is seen by its
works ; for the whole method of life has been devised by
it and ordered, and by it is held together. In like manner
we must think also about the Deity, who in power is
most mighty, in beauty most comely, in life immortal,
and in virtue supreme : wherefore though he is invisible
to human nature, he is seen by his very works." Other
passages to the same purpose are quoted by Gataker,
(p. 382.) Bishop Butler has the same as to the soul :
" Upon the whole then our organs of sense and our limbs
are certainly instruments, which the living persons, ourselves, make use of to perceive and move with." If this
is not plain enough, he also says : "It follows that our
organized bodies are no more ourselves, or part of ourselves, than any other matter around us." (Compare
Anton. x. 38.)

ing to partake of it the intelligent power which
holds within it all things is diffused as wide and
free as the air. (VIII. 54.) It is by living a
divine life that man approaches to a knowledge
of the divinity.[13] It is by following the divinity
within, δαίμων or θεός as Antoninus calls it, that
man comes nearest to the Deity, the supreme good,
for man can never attain to perfect agreement
with his internal guide (τὸ ἡγεμονικόν). " Live
with the gods. And he does live with the gods
who constantly shows to them that his own soul is
satisfied with that which is assigned to him, and
that it does all the daemon (δαίμων) wishes, which
Zeus hath given to every man for his guardian
and guide, a portion of himself. And this daemon
is every man's understanding and reason." (v. 27.)

There is in man, that is in the reason, the intelligence, a superior faculty which if it is exercised rules all the rest. This is the ruling faculty
(τὸ ἡγεμονικόν), which Cicero (De Natura Deo-
rum, II. 11) renders by the Latin word Principatus,
" to which nothing can or ought to be superior."

[13] The reader may consult Discourse V. " Of the existence and nature of God," in John Smith's " Select
Discourses." He has prefixed as a text to this Discourse,
the striking passage of Agapetus, Paraenes. § 3: " He
who knows himself will know God ; and he who knows
God will be made like to God ; and he will be made like
to God, who has become worthy of God ; and he becomes
worthy of God, who does nothing unworthy of God, but
thinks the things that are his, and speaks what he thinks,
and does what he speaks." I suppose that the old saying, " Know thyself," which is attributed to Socrates and
others, had a larger meaning than the narrow sense which
is generally given to it.

Antoninus often uses this term, and others which are equivalent. He names it (VII. 64) "the governing intelligence." The governing faculty is the master of the soul. (v. 26.) A man must reverence only his ruling faculty and the divinity within him. As we must reverence that which is supreme in the universe, so we must reverence that which is supreme in ourselves, and this is that which is of like kind with that which is supreme in the universe. (v. 21.) So, as Plotinus says, the soul of man can only know the divine, so far as it knows itself. In one passage (XI. 19) Antoninus speaks of a man's condemnation of himself, when the diviner part within him has been overpowered and yields to the less honorable and to the perishable part, the body, and its gross pleasures. In a word, the views of Antoninus on this matter, however his expressions may vary, are exactly what Bishop Butler expresses, when he speaks of "the natural supremacy of reflection or conscience," of the faculty " which surveys, approves or disapproves the several affections of our mind and actions of our lives."

Much matter might be collected from Antoninus on the notion of the Universe being one animated Being. But all that he says amounts to no more, as Schultz remarks, than this : the soul of man is most intimately united to his body and together they make one animal, which we call man ; so the Deity is most intimately united to the world or the material universe, and together they form one whole. But Antoninus did not

view God and the material universe as the same,
any more than he viewed the body and soul of
man as one. Antoninus has no speculations on
the absolute nature of the Deity. It was not his
fashion to waste his time on what man cannot
understand. He was satisfied that God exists,
that he governs all things, that man can only have
an imperfect knowledge of his nature, and he must
attain this imperfect knowledge by reverencing
the divinity which is within him, and keeping it
pure.

From all that has been said it follows that the
universe is administered by the Providence of God
(πρόνοια), and that all things are wisely ordered.
There are passages in which Antoninus expresses
doubts, or states different possible theories of the
constitution and government of the Universe, but
he always recurs to his fundamental principle, that
if we admit the existence of a Deity, we must
also admit that he orders all things wisely and
well. (IV. 27 ; VI. 1 ; IX. 28 ; XII. 5, and many
other passages.) Epictetus says (I. 6) that we
can discern the providence which rules the world,
if we possess two things, the power of seeing all
that happens with respect to each thing, and a
grateful disposition.

But if all things are wisely ordered, how is the
world so full of what we call evil, physical and
moral ? If instead of saying that there is evil in
the world, we use the expression which I have
used, " what we call evil," we have partly antici-
pated the Emperor's answer. We see and feel

and know imperfectly very few things in the few
years that we live, and all the knowledge and all
the experience of all the human race is positive
ignorance of the whole, which is infinite. Now
as our reason teaches us that everything is in some
way related to and connected with every other
thing, all notion of evil as being in the universe
of things is a contradiction, for if the whole comes
from and is governed by an intelligent being, it
is impossible to conceive anything in it which tends
to the evil or destruction of the whole. (VIII. 55 ;
x. 6.) Everything is in constant mutation, and
yet the whole subsists. We might imagine the
solar system resolved into its elemental parts, and
yet the whole would still subsist " ever young and
perfect."

All things, all forms, are dissolved and new
forms appear. All living things undergo the
change which we call death. If we call death an
evil, then all change is an evil. Living beings
also suffer pain, and man suffers most of all, for
he suffers both in and by his body and by his
intelligent part. Men suffer also from one another,
and perhaps the largest part of human suffering
comes to man from those whom he calls his broth-
ers. Antoninus says (VIII. 55), " Generally,
wickedness does no harm at all to the universe ;
and particularly, the wickedness [of one man] does
no harm to another. It is only harmful to him
who has it in his power to be released from it, as
soon as he shall choose." The first part of this
is perfectly consistent with the doctrine that the

whole can sustain no evil or harm. The second part must be explained by the Stoic principle that there is no evil in anything which is not in our power. What wrong we suffer from another is his evil, not ours. But this is an admission that there is evil in a sort, for he who does wrong does evil, and if others can endure the wrong, still there is evil in the wrongdoer. Antoninus (XI. 18) gives many excellent precepts with respect to wrongs and injuries, and his precepts are practical. He teaches us to bear what we cannot avoid, and his lessons may be just as useful to him who denies the being and the government of God as to him who believes in both. There is no direct answer in Antoninus to the objections which may be made to the existence and providence of God because of the moral disorder and suffering which are in the world, except this answer which he makes in reply to the supposition that even the best men may be extinguished by death. He says if it is so, we may be sure that if it ought to have been otherwise, the gods would have ordered it otherwise. (XII. 5.) His conviction of the wisdom which we may observe in the government of the world is too strong to be disturbed by any apparent irregularities in the order of things. That these disorders exist is a fact, and those who would conclude from them against the being and government of God conclude too hastily. We all admit that there is an order in the material world, a Nature, in the sense in which that word has been explained, a constitution (κατασκευή.) what

we call a system, a relation of parts to one another
and a fitness of the whole for something. So in
the constitution of plants and of animals there is
an order, a fitness for some end. Sometimes the
order, as we conceive it, is interrupted and the
end, as we conceive it, is not attained. The seed,
the plant or the animal sometimes perishes before
it has passed through all its changes and done all
its uses. It is according to Nature, that is a fixed
order, for some to perish early and for others to
do all their uses and leave successors to take their
place. So man has a corporeal and intellectual
and moral constitution fit for certain uses, and
on the whole man performs these uses, dies and
leaves other men in his place. So society exists,
and a social state is manifestly the Natural State
of man, the state for which his Nature fits him;
and society amidst innumerable irregularities and
disorders still subsists; and perhaps we may say
that the history of the past and our present knowledge give us a reasonable hope that its disorders
will diminish, and that order, its governing principle, may be more firmly established. As order
then, a fixed order, we may say, subject to devia-
tions real or apparent, must be admitted to exist
in the whole Nature of things, that which we call
disorder or evil as it seems to us, does not in any
way alter the fact of the general constitution of
things having a Nature or fixed order. Nobody
will conclude from the existence of disorder that
order is not the rule, for the existence of order
both physical and moral is proved by daily ex-

perience and all past experience. We cannot
conceive how the order of the universe is maintained: we cannot even conceive how our own
life from day to day is continued, nor how we
perform the simplest movements of the body, nor
how we grow and think and act, though we know
many of the conditions which are necessary for
all these functions. Knowing nothing then of
the unseen power which acts in ourselves except
by what is done, we know nothing of the power
which acts through what we call all time and all
space ; but seeing that there is a Nature or fixed
order in all things known to us, it is conformable
to the nature of our minds to believe that this
universal Nature has a cause which operates continually, and that we are totally unable to specu-
late on the reason of any of those disorders or
evils which we perceive. This I believe is the
answer which may be collected from all that Antoninus has said.[14]

The origin of evil is an old question. Achilles
tells Priam (Iliad, 24, 527) that Zeus has two casks,
one filled with good things, and the other with
bad, and that he gives to men out of each according to his pleasure ; and so we must be content,
for we cannot alter the will of Zeus. One of the
Greek commentators asks how must we reconcile
this doctrine with what we find in the first book
of the Odyssey, where the king of the gods says,

[14] Cleanthes says in his Hymn :
" For all things good and bad to One thou formest,
So that One everlasting reason governs all."

5

Men say that evil comes to them from us, but they bring it on themselves through their own folly. The answer is plain enough even to the Greek commentator. The poets make both Achilles and Zeus speak appropriately to their several characters. Indeed Zeus says plainly that men do attribute their sufferings to the gods, but they do it falsely, for they are the cause of their own sorrows.

Epictetus in his Enchiridion (c. 27) makes short work of the question of evil. He says, " As a mark is not set up for the purpose of missing it, so neither does the nature of evil exist in the Universe." This will appear obscure enough to those who are not acquainted with Epictetus, but he always knows what he is talking about. We do not set up a mark in order to miss it, though we may miss it. God, whose existence Epictetus assumes, has not ordered all things so that his purpose shall fail. Whatever there may be of what we call evil, the Nature of evil, as he expresses it, does not exist; that is, evil is not a part of the constitution or nature of Things. If there were a principle of evil (ἀρχή) in the constitution of things, evil would no longer be evil, as Simplicius argues, but evil would be good. Simplicius (c. 34, [27]) has a long and curious discourse on this text of Epictetus, and it is amusing and instructive.

One passage more will conclude this matter. It contains all that the emperor could say (II. 11) : " To go from among men, if there are gods, is not a thing to be afraid of, for the gods will not involve thee in evil ; but if indeed they do not

exist, or if they have no concern about human
affairs, what is it to me to live in a universe devoid
of gods or devoid of providence? But in truth
they do exist, and they do care for human things,
and they have put all the means in man's power
to enable him not to fall into real evils. And as
to the rest, if there was anything evil, they would
have provided for this also, that it should be altogether in a man's power not to fall into it. But
that which does not make a man worse, how can
it make a man's life worse? But neither through
ignorance, nor having the knowledge, but not the
power to guard against or correct these things, is
it possible that the nature of the Universe has
overlooked them; nor is it possible that it has
made so great a mistake, either through want of
power or want of skill, that good and evil should
happen indiscriminately to the good and the bad.
But death certainly and life, honor and dishonor,
pain and pleasure, all these things equally happen
to good and bad men, being things which make
us neither better nor worse. Therefore they are
neither good nor evil."

The Ethical part of Antoninus' Philosophy follows from his general principles. The end of all
his philosophy is to live conformably to Nature,
both a man's own nature and the nature of the
Universe. Bishop Butler has explained what the
Greek philosophers meant when they spoke of
living according to Nature, and he says that when
it is explained, as he has explained it and as they
understood it, it is "a manner of speaking not loose

and undeterminate, but clear and distinct, strictly just and true." To live according to Nature is to live according to a man's whole nature, not according to a part of it, and to reverence the divinity within him as the governor of all his actions. " To the rational animal the same act is according to nature and according to reason." [15] (VII. 11.) That which is done contrary to reason is also an act contrary to nature, to the whole nature, though it is certainly conformable to some part of man's nature, or it could not be done. Man is made for action, not for idleness or pleasure. As plants and animals do the uses of their nature, so man must do his. (V. 1.)

Man must also live conformably to the universal nature, conformably to the nature of all things of which he is one; and as a citizen of a political community he must direct his life and actions with reference to those among whom, and for whom, among other purposes, he lives. A man must not retire into solitude and cut himself off from his fellow men. He must be ever active to do his part in the great whole. All men are his kin, not only in blood, but still more by participating in the same intelligence and by being a portion of the same divinity. A man cannot really be injured by his brethren, for no act of theirs can make him bad, and he must not be angry with them nor hate them : " For we are made for co-

[15] This is what Juvenal means when he says (XIV. 321) —

Nunquam aliud Natura aliud Sapentia dicit

operation, like feet, like hands, like eyelids, like the rows of the upper and lower teeth. To act against one another then is contrary to nature ; and it is acting against one another to be vexed and to turn away." (II. 1.)

Further he says : " Take pleasure in one thing and rest in it, in passing from one social act to another social act, thinking of God." (VI. 7.) Again : " Love mankind. Follow God." (VII. 31.) It is the characteristic of the rational soul for a man to love his neighbor. (XI. 1.) Antoninus teaches in various passages the forgiveness of injuries, and we know that he also practised what he taught. Bishop Butler remarks that " this divine precept to forgive injuries and to love our enemies, though to be met with in Gentile moralists, yet is in a peculiar sense a precept of Christianity, as our Saviour has insisted more upon it than on any other single virtue." The practice of this precept is the most difficult of all virtues. Antoninus often enforces it and gives us aid towards following it. When we are injured, we feel anger and resentment, and the feeling is natural, just and useful for the conservation of society. It is useful that wrong doers should feel the natural consequences of their actions, among which is the disapprobation of society and the re-sentment of him who is wronged. But revenge in the proper sense of that word, must not be prac-tised. " The best way of avenging thyself," says the emperor, " is not to become like the wrong doer." It is plain by this that he does not mean

that we should in any case practise revenge ; but
he says to those who talk of revenging wrongs,
Be not like him who has done the wrong.   Socrates in the Crito (c. 10) says the same in other
words, and St. Paul (Ep. to the Romans, xii. 17.)
" When a man has done thee any wrong, immediately consider with what opinion about good or
evil he has done wrong.   For when thou hast
seen this, thou wilt pity him and wilt neither
wonder nor be angry." (vii. 26.)   Antoninus
would not deny that wrong naturally produces the
feeling of anger and resentment, for this is implied
in the recommendation to reflect on the nature of
the man's mind who has done the wrong, and then
you will have pity instead of resentment : and so
it comes to the same as St. Paul's advice to be
angry and sin not ; which, as Butler well explains
it, is not a recommendation to be angry, which
nobody needs, for anger is a natural passion, but
it is a warning against allowing anger to lead us
into sin.   In short the emperor's doctrine about
wrongful acts is this : wrong doers do not know
what good and bad are : they offend out of ignorance, and in the sense of the Stoics this is true.
Though this kind of ignorance will never be admitted as a legal excuse, and ought not to be
admitted as a full excuse in any way by society,
there may be grievous injuries, such as it is in a
man's power to forgive without harm to society ;
and if he forgives because he sees that his enemies
know not what they do, he is acting in the spirit
of the sublime prayer, " Father, forgive them, for
they know not what they do."

The emperor's moral philosophy was not a feeble, narrow system, which teaches a man to look directly to his own happiness, though a man's happiness or tranquillity is indirectly promoted by living as he ought to do. A man must live conformably to the universal nature, which means, as the emperor explains it in many passages, that a man's actions must be conformable to his true relations to all other human beings, both as a citizen of a political community and as a member of the whole human family. This implies, and he often expresses it in the most forcible language, that a man's words and actions, so far as they affect others, must be measured by a fixed rule, which is their consistency with the conservation and the interests of the particular society of which he is a member, and of the whole human race. To live conformably to such a rule, a man must use his rational faculties in order to discern clearly the consequences and full effect of all his actions and of the actions of others : he must not live a life of contemplation and reflection only, though he must often retire within himself to calm and purify his soul by thought, but he must mingle in the work of man and be a fellow laborer for the general good.

A man should have an object or purpose in life, that he may direct all his energies to it; of course a good object. (II. 7.)   He who has not one object or purpose of life, cannot be one and the same all through his life. (XI. 21.)   Bacon has a remark to the same effect, on the best means of "reducing of the mind unto virtue and good estate ; which

is, the electing and propounding unto a man's self
good and virtuous ends of his life, such as may be
in a reasonable sort within his compass to attain."
He is a happy man who has been wise enough
to do this when he was young and has had the
opportunities; but the emperor seeing well that a
man cannot always be so wise in his youth, encourages himself to do it when he can, and not to
let life slip away before he has begun. He who
can propose to himself good and virtuous ends of
life, and be true to them, cannot fail to live conformably to his own interest and the universal interest, for in the nature of things they are one.
If a thing is not good for the hive, it is not good
for the bee. (vi. 54.)

One passage may end this matter. " If the gods
have determined about me and about the things
which must happen to me, they have determined
well, for it is not easy even to imagine a deity
without forethought; and as to doing me harm,
why should they have any desire towards that?
For what advantage would result to them from
this or to the whole, which is the special object of
their providence? But if they have not determined about me individually, they have certainly
determined about the whole at least; and the
things which happen by way of sequence in this
general arrangement I ought to accept with pleasure and to be content with them. But if they
determine about nothing — which it is wicked to
believe, or if we do believe it, let us neither sacrifice nor pray nor swear by them nor do anything

else which we do as if the gods were present and
lived with us — but if however the gods determine
about none of the things which concern us, I am
able to determine about myself, and I can inquire
about that which is useful; and that is useful to
every man which is conformable to his own constitution (κατασκευή) and nature. But my nature
is rational and social; and my city and country,
so far as I am Antoninus, is Rome; but so far as
I am a man, it is the world. The things then
which are useful to these cities are alone useful
to me." (VI. 44.)

It would be tedious, and it is not necessary to
state the emperor's opinions on all the ways in
which a man may profitably use his understanding
towards perfecting himself in practical virtue.
The passages to this purpose are in all parts of
his book, but as they are in no order or connection, a man must use the book a long time before
he will find out all that is in it. A few words
may be added here. If we analyse all other
things, we find how insufficient they are for human
life, and how truly worthless many of them are.
Virtue alone is indivisible, one, and perfectly satis-
fying. The notion of Virtue cannot be considered
vague or unsettled, because a man may find it
difficult to explain the notion fully to himself or
to expound it to others in such a way as to prevent
cavilling. Virtue is a whole, and no more consists
of parts than man's intelligence does, and yet we
speak of various intellectual faculties as a conven-
ient way of expressing the various powers which

man's intellect shows by its works. In the same
way we may speak of various virtues or parts of
virtue, in a practical sense, for the purpose of
showing what particular virtues we ought to practise in order to the exercise of the whole of virtue,
that is, as much as man's nature is capable of.

The prime principle in man's constitution is
social. The next in order is not to yield to the persuasions of the body, when they are not conformable
to the rational principle, which must govern. The
third is freedom from error and from deception.
" Let then the ruling principle holding fast to
these things go straight on and it has what is its
own." (VII. 55.) The emperor selects justice as
the virtue which is the basis of all the rest (x. 11),
and this had been said long before his time.

It is true that all people have some notion of
what is meant by justice as a disposition of the
mind, and some notion about acting in conformity
to this disposition ; but experience shows that
men's notions about justice are as confused as their
actions are inconsistent with the true notion of
justice. The emperor's notion of justice is clear
enough, but not practical enough for all mankind.
" Let there be freedom from perturbations with
respect to the things which come from the external cause ; and let there be justice in the things
done by virtue of the internal cause, that is, let
there be movement and action terminating in this,
in social acts, for this is according to thy nature."
(IX. 31.) In another place (IX. 1) he says that
" he who acts unjustly acts impiously," which fol-

lows of course from all that he says in various
places. He insists on the practice of truth as a
virtue and as a means to virtue, which no doubt
it is : for lying even in indifferent things weakens
the understanding; and lying maliciously is as
great a moral offence as a man can be guilty of,
viewed both as showing an habitual disposition,
and viewed with respect to its consequences. He
couples the notion of justice with action. A man
must not pride himself on having some fine notion
of justice in his head, but he must exhibit his
justice in act, like St. James's notion of faith.
But this is enough.

The Stoics and Antoninus among them call some
things beautiful (καλά) and some ugly (αἰσχρά),
and as they are beautiful so they are good, and as
they are ugly so they are evil or bad. (II. 1.) All
these things good and evil are in our power,
absolutely some of the stricter Stoics would say;
in a manner only, as those who would not depart
altogether from common sense would say; practi-
cally they are to a great degree in the power of
some persons and in some circumstances, but in a
small degree only in other persons and in other
circumstances. The Stoics maintain man's free
will as to the things which are in his power; for
as to the things which are out of his power, free
will terminating in action is of course excluded
by the very terms of the expression. I hardly
know if we can discover exactly Antoninus' notion
of the free will of man, nor is the question worth
the inquiry. What he does mean and does say is

intelligible. All the things which are not in our power (ἀπροαίρετα) are indifferent: they are neither good nor bad, morally. Such are life, health, wealth, power, disease, poverty and death. Life and death are all men's portion. Health, wealth, power, disease and poverty happen to men indifferently to the good and to the bad; to those who live according to nature and to those who do not. "Life," says the emperor, "is a warfare and a stranger's sojourn, and after fame is oblivion." (II. 17.) After speaking of those men who have disturbed the world and then died, and of the death of philosophers such as Heraclitus and Democritus who was destroyed by lice, and of Socrates whom other lice (his enemies) destroyed, he says: " What means all this? Thou hast embarked, thou hast made the voyage, thou art come to shore; get out. If indeed to another life, there is no want of gods, not even there. But if to a state without sensation, thou wilt cease to be held by pains and pleasures, and to be a slave to the vessel which is as much inferior as that which serves it is superior: for the one is intelligence and deity; the other is earth and corruption." (III. 3.) It is not death that a man should fear, but he should fear never beginning to live according to nature. (XII. 1.) Every man should live in such a way as to discharge his duty, and to trouble himself about nothing else. He should live such a life that he shall always be ready for death, and shall depart content when the summons comes. For what is death? " A cessation of the impressions

through the senses, and of the pulling of the strings
which move the appetites and of the discursive
movements of the thoughts, and of the service to
the flesh." (vi. 28.) Death is such as generation
is, a mystery of nature. (iv. 5.) In another
passage, the exact meaning of which is perhaps
doubtful (ix. 3), he speaks of the child which
leaves the womb, and so he says the soul at death
leaves its envelope. As the child is born or comes
into life by leaving the womb, so the soul may on
leaving the body pass into another existence which
is perfect. I am not sure if this is the emperor's
meaning. Butler compares it with a passage in
Strabo about the Brahmins' notion of death being
the birth into real life and a happy life to those
who have philosophized ; and he thinks that Antoninus may allude to this opinion.[16]

Antoninus' opinion of a future life is nowhere
clearly expressed. His doctrine of the nature of
the soul of necessity implies that it does not perish
absolutely, for a portion of the divinity cannot
perish. The opinion is at least as old as the time
of Epicharmus and Euripides ; what comes from
earth goes back to earth, and what comes from
heaven, the divinity, returns to him who gave it.
But I find nothing clear in Antoninus as to the

[16] Seneca (Ep. 102) has the same, whether an expression of his own opinion, or merely a fine saying of others
employed to embellish his writings, I know not. After
speaking of the child being prepared in the womb to live
this life, he adds, " Sic per hoc spatium, quod ab infantia
patet in senectutem, in alium naturae sumimur partum.
Alia origo nos expectat, alius rerum status."

notion of the man existing after death so as to be
conscious of his sameness with that soul which
occupied his vessel of clay.   He seems to be
perplexed on this matter, and finally to have rested
in this, that God or the gods will do whatever is
best and consistent with the university of things.

Nor I think does he speak conclusively on
another Stoic doctrine, which some Stoics practised, the anticipating the regular course of nature
by a man's own act.   The reader will find some
passages in which this is touched on, and he may
make of them what he can.   But there are passages in which the emperor encourages himself to
wait for the end patiently and with tranquillity;
and certainly it is consistent with all his best
teaching that a man should bear all that falls to
his lot and do useful acts as long as he lives.   He
should not therefore abridge the time of his use-
fulness by his own act.   Whether he contemplates
any possible cases in which a man should die by
his own hand, I cannot tell, and the matter is not
worth a curious inquiry, for I believe it would not
lead to any certain result as to his opinion on this
point.   I do not think that Antoninus, who never
mentions Seneca, though he must have known all
about him, would have agreed with Seneca when
he gives as a reason for suicide, that the eternal
law, whatever he means, has made nothing better
for us than this, that it has given us only one way
of entering into life and many ways of going out
of it.   The ways of going out indeed are many,
and that is a good reason for a man taking care
of himself.

Happiness was not the direct object of a Stoic's life. There is no rule of life contained in the precept that a man should pursue his own happiness. Many men think that they are seeking happiness when they are only seeking the gratification of some particular passion, the strongest that they have. The end of a man is, as already explained, to live conformably to nature, and he will thus obtain happiness, tranquillity of mind and contentment. (III. 12 ; VIII. 1. and other places.) As a means of living conformably to nature he must study the four chief virtues, each of which has its proper sphere : wisdom or the knowledge of good and evil ; justice, or the giving to every man his due ; fortitude, or the enduring of labor and pain ; and temperance, which is moderation in all things. By thus living conformably to nature, the Stoic obtained all that he wished or expected. His reward was in his virtuous life, and he was satisfied with that. Some Greek poet long ago wrote : —

> For virtue only of all human things
> Takes her reward not from the hands of others.
> Virtue herself rewards the toils of virtue.

Some of the Stoics indeed expressed themselves in very arrogant, absurd terms, about the wise man's self sufficiency ; they elevated him to the rank of a deity.[17] But these were only talkers

[17] J. Smith in his Select Discourses on " the Excellency and Nobleness of true religion " (c. VI.) has remarked on this Stoical arrogance. He finds it in Seneca and others. In Seneca certainly, and perhaps something of it in Epictetus ; but it is not in Antoninus.

and lecturers, such as those in all ages who utter
fine words, know little of human affairs, and care
only for notoriety. Epictetus and Antoninus both
by precept and example labored to improve themselves and others; and if we discover imperfec-
tions in their teaching, we must still honor these
great men who attempted to show that there is in
man's nature and in the constitution of things
sufficient reason for living a virtuous life. It is
difficult enough to live as we ought to live, difficult even for any man to live in such a way as to
satisfy himself, if he exercises only in a moderate
degree the power of reflecting upon and reviewing
his own conduct; and if all men cannot be brought
to the same opinions in morals and religion, it is
at least worth while to give them good reasons for
as much as they can be persuaded to accept.

M. ANTONINUS.

I.

ROM my grandfather Verus[1] [I learned] good morals and the government of my temper.

2. From the reputation and remembrance of my father,[2] modesty and a manly character.

[1] Annius Verus was his grandfather's name. There is no verb in this section connected with the word " from," nor in the following sections of this book ; and it is not quite certain what verb should be supplied. What I have added may express the meaning here, though there are sections which it will not fit. If he does not mean to say that he learned all these good things from the several persons whom he mentions, he means that he observed certain good qualities in them, or received certain benefits from them, and it is implied that he was the better for it, or at least might have been ; for it would be a mistake to understand Marcus as saying that he possessed all the virtues which he observed in his kinsmen and teachers.

[2] His father's name was Annius Verus.

6

3. From my mother,[3] piety and beneficence, and abstinence, not only from evil deeds, but even from evil thoughts; and further, simplicity in my way of living, far removed from the habits of the rich.

4. From my great-grandfather,[4] not to have frequented public schools, and to have had good teachers at home, and to know that on such things a man should spend liberally.

5. From my governor, to be neither of the green nor of the blue party at the games in the Circus, nor a partisan either of the Parmularius or the Scutarius at the gladiators' fights; from him too I learned endurance of labor, and to want little, and to work with my own hands, and not to meddle with other people's affairs, and not to be ready to listen to slander.

6. From Diognetus, not to busy myself about trifling things, and not to give credit to what was said by miracle-workers and jugglers about incantations and the driving away of daemons and such things; and not to breed quails [for fighting], nor to give myself up passionately to such things; and to endure freedom of speech; and to have become

[3] His mother was Domitia Calvilla, named also Lucilla.

[4] Perhaps his mother's grandfather, Catilius Severus.

intimate with philosophy; and to have been a hearer, first of Bacchius, then of Tandasis and Marcianus; and to have written dialogues in my youth; and to have desired a plank bed and skin, and whatever else of the kind belongs to the Grecian discipline.

7. From Rusticus [5] I received the impression that my character required improvement and discipline; and from him I learned not to be led astray to sophistic emulation, nor to writing on speculative matters, nor to delivering little hortatory orations, nor to showing myself off as a man who practises much discipline, or does benevolent acts in order to make a display; and to abstain from rhetoric, and poetry, and fine writing; and not to walk about in the house in my outdoor dress, nor to do other things of the kind; and to write my letters with simplicity, like the letter

[5] Q. Junius Rusticus was a Stoic philosopher, whom Antoninus valued highly, and often took his advice. (Capitol. *M. Antonin.* iii.)

Antoninus says, τοῖς 'Επικτητείοις ὑπομνήμασιν, which must not be translated, "the writings of Epictetus," for Epictetus wrote nothing. His pupil Arrian, who has preserved for us all that we know of Epictetus, says, ταῦτα ἐπειράθην ὑπομνήματα ἐμαυτῷ διαφυλάξαι τῆς ἐκείνου διανοίας. (*Ep. ad Gell.*)

which Rusticus wrote from Sinuessa to my moth
er ; and with respect to those who have offended
me by words, or done me wrong, to be easily disposed to be pacified and reconciled, as soon as they
have shown a readiness to be reconciled ; and to
read carefully, and not to be satisfied with a su-
perficial understanding of a book ; nor hastily to
give my assent to those who talk over-much ; and
I am indebted to him for being acquainted with
the discourses of Epictetus, which he communi-
cated to me out of his own collection.

8. From Apollonius [6] I learned freedom of will
and undeviating steadiness of purpose ; and to
look to nothing else, not even for a moment, except to reason ; and to be always the same, in
sharp pains, on the occasion of the loss of a child,
and in long illness ; and to see clearly in a living
example that the same man can be both most res-
olute and yielding, and not peevish in giving his
instruction ; and to have had before my eyes a
man who clearly considered his experience and his
skill in expounding philosophical principles as the
smallest of his merits ; and from him I learned
how to receive from friends what are esteemed

---

[6] Apollonius of Chalcis came to Rome in the time of
Pius to be Marcus' preceptor. He was a rigid Stoic.

favors, without being either humbled by them or letting them pass unnoticed.

9. From Sextus,[7] a benevolent disposition, and the example of a family governed in a fatherly manner, and the idea of living conformably to nature; and gravity without affectation, and to look carefully after the interests of friends, and to tolerate ignorant persons, and those who form opinions without consideration † : he had the power of readily accommodating himself to all, so that intercourse with him was more agreeable than any flattery; and at the same time he was most highly venerated by those who associated with him: and he had the faculty both of discovering and ordering, in an intelligent and methodical way, the principles necessary for life; and he never showed anger or any other passion, but was entirely free from passion, and also most affectionate; and he could express approbation without noisy display, and he possessed much knowledge without ostentation.

10. From Alexander[8] the grammarian, to refrain from fault-finding, and not .in a reproachful

---

[7] Sextus of Chæronea, a grandson of Plutarch, or nephew, as some say; but more probably a grandson.

[8] Alexander was a Grammaticus, a native of Phrygia. He wrote a commentary on Homer; and the rhetorician

way to chide those who uttered any barbarous or
solecistic or strange-sounding expression ; but dex-
terously to introduce the very expression which
ought to have been used, and in the way of answer
or giving confirmation, or joining in an inquiry
about the thing itself, not about the word, or by
some other fit suggestion.

11. From Fronto[9] I learned to observe what
envy, and duplicity, and hypocrisy are in a tyrant,
and that generally those among us who are called
Patricians are rather deficient in paternal affection.

12. From Alexander the Platonic, not frequently nor without necessity to say to any one, or to
write in a letter, that I have no leisure ; nor continually to excuse the neglect of duties required
by our relation to those with whom we live, by
alleging urgent occupations.

13. From Catulus,[10] not to be indifferent when
a friend finds fault, even if he should find fault
without reason, but to try to restore him to his
usual disposition ; and to be ready to speak well

Aristides wrote a panegyric on Alexander in a funeral
oration.

[9] Cornelius Fronto was a rhetorician, and in great
favor with Marcus. There are extant various letters
between Marcus and Fronto.

[10] Cinna Catulus, a Stoic philosopher.

of teachers, as it is reported of Domitius and
Athenodotus; and to love my children truly.

14. From my brother [11] Severus, to love my
kin, and to love truth, and to love justice; and
through him I learned to know Thrasea, Helvidius, Cato, Dion, Brutus; [12] and from him I received the idea of a polity in which there is the same
law for all, a polity administered with regard to
equal rights and equal freedom of speech, and the
idea of a kingly government which respects most
of all the freedom of the governed; I learned from
him also † consistency and undeviating steadiness
in my regard for philosophy; and a disposition to
do good, and to give to others readily, and to cherish good hopes, and to believe that I am loved by
my friends; and in him I observed no conceal-
ment of his opinions with respect to those whom

[11] The word brother may not be genuine. Antoninus
had no brother. It has been supposed that he may
mean some cousin. Schultz omits "brother," and says
that this Severus is probably Claudius Severus, a peri-
patetic.

[12] We know, from Tacitus (*Annal.* xiii., xvi. 21; and
other passages), who Thrasea and Helvidius were. Plutarch has written the lives of the two Catos, and of
Dion and Brutus. Antoninus probably alludes to Cato
of Utica, who was a Stoic.

he condemned, and that his friends had no need
to conjecture what he wished or did not wish,
but it was quite plain.

15. From Maximus[13] I learned self-government,
and not to be led aside by anything; and cheer-
fulness in all circumstances, as well as in illness;
and a just admixture in the moral character of
sweetness and dignity, and to do what was set
before me without complaining. I observed that
everybody believed that he thought as he spoke,
and that in all that he did he never had any bad
intention; and he never showed amazement and
surprise, and was never in a hurry, and never put
off doing a thing, nor was perplexed nor dejected,
nor did he ever laugh to disguise his vexation, nor,
on the other hand, was he ever passionate or suspicious. He was accustomed to do acts of beneficence, and was ready to forgive, and was free from
all falsehood; and he presented the appearance
of a man who could not be diverted from right
rather than of a man who had been improved. I
observed, too, that no man could ever think that

---

[13] Claudius Maximus was a Stoic philosopher, who
was highly esteemed also by Antoninus Pius, Marcus'
predecessor. The character of Maximus is that of a
perfect man. (See viii. 25.)

he was despised by Maximus, or ever venture to think himself a better man.   He had also the art of being humorous in an agreeable way.†

16. In my father[14] I observed mildness of temper, and unchangeable resolution in the things which he had determined after due deliberation; and no vainglory in those things which men call honors; and a love of labor and perseverance; and a readiness to listen to those who had anything to propose for the common weal; and undeviating firmness in giving to every man according to his deserts; and a knowledge derived from experience of the occasions for vigorous action and for remission. And I observed that he had overcome all passion for boys; and he considered himself no more than any other citizen; and he released his friends from all obligation to sup with him or to attend him of necessity when he went abroad, and those who had failed to accompany him, by reason of any urgent circumstances, always found him the same.   I observed too his habit of careful inquiry in all matters of deliberation, and his persistency, and that he never stopped his investigation through being satisfied with appearances which first present

[14] He means his adoptive father, his predecessor, the Emperor Antoninus Pius.

themselves ; and that his disposition was to keep
his friends, and not to be soon tired of them, nor
yet to be extravagant in his affection; and to be
satisfied on all occasions, and cheerful ; and to
foresee things a long way off, and to provide for the
smallest without display ; and to check immediately
popular applause and all flattery ; and to be ever
watchful over the things which were necessary for
the administration of the empire, and to be a good
manager of the expenditure, and patiently to endure the blame which he got for such conduct;
and he was neither superstitious with respect to
the gods, nor did he court men by gifts or by trying to please them, or by flattering the populace ;
but he showed sobriety in all things and firmness,
and never any mean thoughts or action, nor love
of novelty.   And the things which conduce in any
way to the commodity of life, and of which fortune
gives an abundant supply, he used without arrogance and without excusing himself ; so that when
he had them, he enjoyed them without affectation,
and when he had them not, he did not want them.
No one could ever say of him that he was either a
sophist or a [home-bred] flippant slave or a pedant ;
but every one acknowledged him to be a man ripe,
perfect, above flattery, able to manage his own and
other men's affairs.   Besides this, he honored

those who were true philosophers, and he did not
reproach those who pretended to be philosophers,
nor yet was he easily led by them. He was also
easy in conversation, and he made himself agreeable without any offensive affectation. He took a
reasonable care of his body's health, not as one who
was greatly attached to life, nor out of regard to
personal appearance, nor yet in a careless way, but
so that, through his own attention, he very seldom
stood in need of the physician's art or of medi-
cine or external applications. He was most ready
to give way without envy to those who possessed
any particular faculty, such as that of eloquence or
knowledge of the law or of morals, or of anything
else ; and he gave them his help, that each might
enjoy reputation according to his deserts ; and he
always acted conformably to the institutions of his
country, without showing any affectation of doing
so. Further, he was not fond of change nor un-
steady, but he loved to stay in the same places, and
to employ himself about the same things ; and
after his paroxysms of headache he came immediately fresh and vigorous to his usual occupations. His secrets were not many, but very few
and very rare, and these only about public matters ; and he showed prudence and economy in the
exhibition of the public spectacles and the con-

struction of public buildings, his donations to the
people, and in such things, for he was a man who
looked to what ought to be done, not to the reputation which is got by a man's acts. He did not
take the bath at unseasonable hours ; he was not
fond of building houses, nor curious about what he
ate, nor about the texture and color of his clothes,
nor about the beauty of his slaves.[15] His dress
came from Lorium, his villa on the coast, and from
Lanuvium generally.[16] We know how he behaved
to the toll-collector in Tusculum who asked his
pardon ; and such was all his behavior. There
was in him nothing harsh, nor implacable, nor
violent, nor, as one may say, anything carried to
the sweating point; but he examined all things
severally, as if he had abundance of time, and without confusion, in an orderly way, vigorously and
consistently. And that might be applied to him
which is recorded of Socrates,[17] that he was able
both to abstain from, and to enjoy, those things
which many are too weak to abstain from, and

[15] This passage is corrupt, and the exact meaning is
uncertain.

[16] Lorium was a villa on the coast north of Rome, and
there Antoninus was brought up, and he died there. This
also is corrupt.

[17] *Xenophon, Memorab.* i. 3. 15.

cannot enjoy without excess. But to be strong enough both to bear the one and to be sober in the other is the mark of a man who has a perfect and invincible soul, such as he showed in the illness of Maximus.

17. To the gods I am indebted for having good grandfathers, good parents, a good sister, good teachers, good associates, good kinsmen and friends, nearly everything good. Further, I owe it to the gods that I was not hurried into any offence against any of them, though I had a disposition which, if opportunity had offered, might have led me to do something of this kind; but, through their favor, there never was such a concurrence of circumstances as put me to the trial. Further, I am thankful to the gods that I was not longer brought up with my grandfather's concubine, and that I preserved the flower of my youth, and that I did not make proof of my virility before the proper season, but even deferred the time; that I was subjected to a ruler and a father who was able to take away all pride from me, and to bring me to the knowledge that it is possible for a man to live in a palace without wanting either guards or embroidered dresses, or torches and statues, and such-like show; but that it is in such a man's power to bring himself very

near to the fashion of a private person, without being for this reason either meaner in thought, or more remiss in action, with respect to the things which must be done for the public interest in a manner that befits a ruler. I thank the gods for giving me such a brother,[18] who was able by his moral character to rouse me to vigilance over myself, and who, at the same time, pleased me by his respect and affection; that my children have not been stupid nor deformed in body; that I did not make more proficiency in rhetoric, poetry, and the other studies, in which I should perhaps have been completely engaged, if I had seen that I was making progress in them; that I made haste to place those who brought me up in the station of honor, which they seemed to desire, without putting them off with hope of my doing it some time after, because they were then still young; that I knew Apollonius, Rusticus, Maximus; that I received clear and frequent impressions about living according to nature, and what kind of a life that is, so that, so far as depended on the gods, and their gifts, and help, and inspirations, nothing hindered me from forthwith living according to nature, though I still fall short of it through my own

[18] The emperor had no brother, except L. Verus, his brother by adoption.

fault, and through not observing the admonitions
of the gods, and, I may almost say, their direct
instructions ; that my body has held out so long
in such a kind of life ; that I never touched either
Benedicta or Theodotus, and that, after having
fallen into amatory passions, I was cured ; and,
though I was often out of humor with Rusticus, I
never did anything of which I had occasion to repent ; that, though it was my mother's fate to die
young, she spent the last years of her life with
me ; that, whenever I wished to help any man in
his need, or on any other occasion, I was never
told that I had not the means of doing it ; and
that to myself the same necessity never happened,
to receive anything from another ; that I have
such a wife,[19] so obedient, and so affectionate, and
so simple ; that I had abundance of good masters
for my children ; and that remedies have been
shown to me by dreams, both others, and against
bloodspitting and giddiness [20] . . . . . . ; and that,
when I had an inclination to philosophy, I did not
fall into the hands of any sophist, and that I did
not waste my time on writers [of histories], or in
the resolution of syllogisms, or occupy myself
about the investigation of appearances in the

[19] See the *Life of Antoninus.*
[20] **This** is corrupt.

heavens ; for all these things require the help
of the gods and fortune.

Among the Quadi at the Granua.[21]

[21] The Quadi lived in the southern part of Bohemia
and Moravia; and Antoninus made a campaign against
them. (See the *Life.*) Granua is probably the river
Graan, which flows into the Danube.

If these words are genuine, Antoninus may have written this first book during the war with the Quadi. In
the first edition of Antoninus, and in the older editions,
the first three sections of the second book make the conclusion of the first book. Gataker placed them at the
beginning of the second book.

II.

EGIN the morning by saying to thy-self, I shall meet with the busybody, the ungrateful, arrogant, deceitful, envious, unsocial. All these things happen to them by reason of their ignorance of what is good and evil. But I who have seen the nature of the good that it is beautiful, and of the bad that it is ugly, and the nature of him who does wrong, that it is akin to me, not [only] of the same blood or seed, but that it participates in [the same] intelligence and [the same] portion of the divinity, I can neither be injured by any of them, for no one can fix on me what is ugly, nor can I be angry with my kinsman, nor hate him. For we are made for co-operation, like feet, like hands, like eyelids, like the rows of the upper and lower teeth. To act against one another then is contrary to nature ; and it is acting against one another to be vexed and to turn away.

2. Whatever this is that I am, it is a little flesh

7

and breath, and the ruling part.   Throw away thy
books ; no longer distract thyself : it is not allowed ;
but as if thou wast now dying, despise the flesh :
it is blood and bones and a network, a contexture
of nerves, veins, and arteries.   See the breath also.
what kind of a thing it is, air, and not always the
same, but every moment sent out and again sucked
in.   The third then is the ruling part : consider
thus :   Thou art an old man ; no longer let this be
a slave, no longer be pulled by the strings like a
puppet to unsocial movements, no longer be either
dissatisfied with thy present lot, or shrink from
the future.

3.   All that is from the gods is full of providence.
That which is from fortune is not separated from
nature or without an interweaving and involution
with the things which are ordered by providence.
From thence all things flow ; and there is besides
necessity, and that which is for the advantage of
the whole universe, of which thou art a part.
But that is good for every part of nature which
the nature of the whole brings, and what serves to
maintain this nature.   Now the universe is preserved, as by the changes of the elements so by the
changes of things compounded.   Let these principles be enough for thee, let them always be
fixed opinions.   But cast away the thirst after

books, that thou mayest not die murmuring, but cheerfully, truly, and from thy heart thankful to the gods.

4. Remember how long thou hast been putting off these things, and how often thou hast received an opportunity from the gods, and yet dost not use it. Thou must now at last perceive of what universe thou art a part, and of what administrator of the universe thy existence is an efflux, and that a limit of time is fixed for thee, which if thou dost not use for clearing away the clouds from thy mind, it will go and thou wilt go, and it will never return.

5. Every moment think steadily as a Roman and a man, to do what thou hast in hand with perfect and simple dignity, and feeling of affection, and freedom, and justice; and to give thyself relief from all other thoughts. And thou wilt give thyself relief, if thou doest every act of thy life as if it were the last, laying aside all carelessness and passionate aversion from the commands of reason, and all hypocrisy, and self-love, and discontent with the portion which has been given to thee. Thou seest how few the things are, the which if a man lays hold of, he is able to live a life which flows in quiet, and is like the existence of the gods; for the gods on their part

will require nothing more from him who observes these things.

6. Do wrong to thyself, do wrong to thyself, my soul; but thou wilt no longer have the opportunity of honoring thyself. Every man's life is sufficient.† But thine is nearly finished, though thy soul reverences not itself, but places thy felicity in the souls of others.

7. Do the things external which fall upon thee distract thee? Give thyself time to learn something new and good, and cease to be whirled around. But then thou must also avoid being carried about the other way. For those too are triflers who have wearied themselves in life by their activity, and yet have no object to which to direct every movement, and, in a word, all their thoughts.

8. Through not observing what is in the mind of another a man has seldom been seen to be unhappy; but those who do not observe the movements of their own minds must of necessity be unhappy.

9. This thou must always bear in mind, what is the nature of the whole, and what is my nature, and how this is related to that, and what kind of a part it is of what kind of a whole; and that there is no one who hinders thee from always

doing and saying the things which are according
to the nature of which thou art a part.

10. Theophrastus, in his comparison of bad acts
— such a comparison as one would make in accord-
ance with the common notions of mankind — says,
like a true philosopher, that the offences which are
committed through desire are more blamable than
those which are committed through anger.   For he
who is excited by anger seems to turn away from
reason with a certain pain and unconscious con-
traction ; but he who offends through desire, being
overpowered by pleasure, seems to be in a manner more intemperate and more womanish in his
offences.   Rightly then, and in a way worthy of
philosophy, he said that the offence which is committed with pleasure is more blamable than that
which is committed with pain ; and on the whole
the one is more like a person who has been first
wronged and through pain is compelled to be
angry ; but the other is moved by his own impulse
to do wrong, being carried towards doing something by desire.

11. [Since it is possible that thou mayest depart
from life this very moment, regulate every act and
thought accordingly.] But to go away from among
men, if there are gods, is not a thing to be afraid
of, for the gods will not involve thee in evil ; but

if indeed they do not exist, or if they have no
concern about human affairs, what is it to me to
live in a universe devoid of gods or devoid of
providence? But in truth they do exist, and they
do care for human things, and they have put all
the means in man's power to enable him not to
fall into real evils. And as to the rest, if there
was anything evil, they would have provided for
this also, that it should be altogether in a man's
power not to fall into it. Now that which does
not make a man worse, how can it make a man's
life worse? But neither through ignorance, nor
having the knowledge, but not the power to guard
against or correct these things, is it possible that
the nature of the universe has overlooked them;
nor is it possible that it has made so great a mistake, either through want of power or want of
skill, that good and evil should happen indiscriminately to the good and the bad. But death certainly, and life, honor and dishonor, pain and pleasure, all these things equally happen to good men
and bad, being things which make us neither better nor worse. Therefore they are neither good
nor evil.

12. How quickly all things disappear, in the
universe? the bodies themselves, but in time the
remembrance of them; what is the nature of all

sensible things, and particularly those which
attract with the bait of pleasure or terrify by
pain, or are noised abroad by vapory fame; how
worthless, and contemptible, and sordid, and perishable, and dead they are — all this it is the
part of the intellectual faculty to observe. To
observe too who these are whose opinions and
voices give reputation; what death is, and the
fact that, if a man looks at it in itself, and by
the abstractive power of reflection resolves into
their parts all the things which present themselves to the imagination in it, he will then consider it to be nothing else than an operation of
nature; and if any one is afraid of an operation of nature, he is a child. This, however, is
not only an operation of nature, but it is also a
thing which conduces to the purposes of nature.
To observe too how man comes near to the deity,
and by what part of him, and when this part of
man is so disposed.†

13. Nothing is more wretched than a man who
traverses everything in a round, and pries into the
things beneath the earth, as the poet says, and
seeks by conjecture what is in the minds of his
neighbors, without perceiving that it is sufficient
to attend to the daemon within him, and to
reverence it sincerely. And reverence of the

daemon consists in keeping it pure from passion
and thoughtlessness, and dissatisfaction with what
comes from gods and men. For the things from
the gods merit veneration for their excellence ;
and the things from men should be dear to us by
reason of kinship; and sometimes even, in a manner, they move our pity by reason of men's ignorance of good and bad; this defect being not less
than that which deprives us of the power of dis-
tinguishing things that are white and black.

14. Though thou shouldest be going to live
three thousand years, and as many times ten
thousand years, still remember that no man loses
any other life than this which he now lives, nor
lives any other than this which he now loses.
The longest and shortest are thus brought to
the same. For the present is the same to all,
though that which is past is not the same ; and
so that which is lost appears to be a mere moment. For a man cannot lose either the past
or the future : for what a man has not, how can
any one take this from him ? These two things
then thou must bear in mind; the one, that all
things from eternity are of like forms and come
round in a circle, and that it makes no difference
whether a man shall see the same things during
a hundred years or two hundred, or an infinite

time ; and the second, that the longest liver and
he who will die soonest lose just the same. For
the present is the only thing of which a man
can be deprived, if it is true that this is the only
thing which he has, and that a man cannot lose
a thing if he has it not.

15. Remember that all is opinion. For what
was said by the Cynic Monimus is manifest : and
manifest too is the use of what was said, if a
man receives what may be got out of it as far
as it is true.

16. The soul of man does violence to itself, first
of all, when it becomes an abscess and, as it were,
a tumor on the universe, so far as it can. For to
be vexed at anything which happens is a separation of ourselves from nature, in some part of
which the natures of all other things are contained. In the next place, the soul does violence to itself when it turns away from any man,
or even moves towards him with the intention
of injuring, such as are the souls of those who
are angry. In the third place, the soul does
violence to itself when it is overpowered by
pleasure or by pain. Fourthly, when it plays
a part, and does or says anything insincerely
and untruly. Fifthly, when it allows any act
of its own and any movement to be without an

aim, and does anything thoughtlessly and without considering what it is, it being right that
even the smallest things be done with reference
to an end ; and the end of rational animals is to
follow the reason and the law of the most ancient city and polity.

17. Of human life the time is a point, and the
substance is in a flux, and the perception dull,
and the composition of the whole body subject
to putrefaction, and the soul a whirl, and fortune hard to divine, and fame a thing devoid of
judgment. And, to say all in a word, everything
which belongs to the body is a stream, and what
belongs to the soul is a dream and vapor, and life
is a warfare and a stranger's sojourn, and after-
fame is oblivion. What then is that which is
able to conduct a man? One thing and only
one, philosophy. But this consists in keeping
the daemon within a man free from violence
and unharmed, superior to pains and pleasures,
doing nothing without a purpose, nor yet falsely
and with hypocrisy, not feeling the need of another man's doing or not doing anything; and
besides, accepting all that happens, and all that
is allotted, as coming from thence, wherever it
is, from whence he himself came ; and, finally,
waiting for death with a cheerful mind, as be-

ing nothing else than a dissolution of the elements of which every living being is compounded.
But if there is no harm to the elements themselves in each continually changing into another,
why should a man have any apprehension about
the change and dissolution of all the elements?
For it is according to nature, and nothing is evil
which is according to nature.

This in Carnuntum.[1]

[1] Carnuntum was a town of Pannonia, on the south
side of the Danube, about thirty miles east of Vindo-
bona (Vienna). Orosius (vii. 15.) and Eutropius (viii.
13.) say that Antoninus remained three years at Carnuntum during his war with the Marcomanni.

III.

E ought to consider not only that our life is daily wasting away and a smaller part of it is left, but another thing also must be taken into the account, that if a man should live longer, it is quite uncertain whether the understanding will still continue sufficient for the comprehension of things, and retain the power of contemplation which strives to acquire the knowledge of the divine and the human. For if he shall begin to fall into dotage, perspiration, and nutrition, and imagination, and appetite, and whatever else there is of the kind, will not fail; but the power of making use of ourselves, and filling up the measure of our duty, and clearly separating all appearances, and considering whether a man should now depart from life, and whatever else of the kind absolutely requires a disciplined reason, all this is already extinguished.

We must make haste then, not only because we
are daily nearer to death, but also because the
conception of things and the understanding of
them cease first.

2. We ought to observe also that even the
things which follow after the things which are
produced according to nature contain something
pleasing and attractive. For instance, when
bread is baked some parts are split at the sur-
face, and these parts which thus open, and have
a certain fashion contrary to the purpose of the
baker's art, are beautiful in a manner, and in a
peculiar way excite a desire for eating. And
again, figs, when they are quite ripe, gape open ;
and in the ripe olives the very circumstance of
their being near to rottenness adds a peculiar
beauty to the fruit. And the ears of corn bend-
ing down, and the lion's eyebrows, and the
foam which flows from the mouth of wild boars,
and many other things — though they are far
from being beautiful, if a man should examine
them severally, — still, because they are con-
sequent upon the things which are formed by
nature, help to adorn them, and they please the
mind ; so that if a man should have a feeling
and deeper insight with respect to the things
which are produced in the universe, there is

hardly one of those which follow by way of consequence which will not seem to him to be in a
manner disposed so as to give pleasure. And so
he will see even the real gaping jaws of wild
beasts with no less pleasure than those which
painters and sculptors show by imitation; and
in an old woman and an old man he will be
able to see a certain maturity and comeliness;
and the attractive loveliness of young persons,
he will be able to look on with chaste eyes;
and many such things will present themselves,
not pleasing to every man, but to him only who
has become truly familiar with nature and her
works.

3. Hippocrates after curing many diseases himself fell sick and died. The Chaldaei foretold
the deaths of many, and then fate caught them
too. Alexander, and Pompeius, and Caius Caesar, after so often completely destroying whole
cities, and in battle cutting to pieces many ten
thousands of cavalry and infantry, themselves
too at last departed from life. Heraclitus, after
so many speculations on the conflagration of the
universe, was filled with water internally and
died smeared all over with mud. And lice destroyed Democritus; and other lice killed Socrates. What means all this? Thou hast em-

barked, thou hast made the voyage, thou art come
to shore; get out. If indeed to another life, there
is no want of gods, not even there. But if to a
state without sensation, thou wilt cease to be
held by pains and pleasures, and to be a slave
to the vessel, which is as much inferior as that
which serves it is superior: † for the one is intelligence and deity; the other is earth and corruption.

4. Do not waste the remainder of thy life in
thoughts about others, when thou dost not refer
thy thoughts to some object of common utility.
For thou losest the opportunity of doing something else when thou hast such thoughts as these.
What is such a person doing, and why, and what
is he saying, and what is he thinking of, and what
is he contriving, and whatever else of the kind
makes us wander away from the observation of
our own ruling power. We ought then to check
in the series of our thoughts everything that is
without a purpose and useless, but most of all
the overcurious feeling and the malignant; and
a man should use himself to think of those
things only about which if one should suddenly
ask, What hast thou now in thy thoughts? with
perfect openness thou mightest immediately answer, This or That; so that from thy words it

should be plain that everything in thee is simple and benevolent, and such as befits a social animal, and one that cares not for thoughts about pleasure or sensual enjoyments at all, or any rivalry or envy and suspicion, or anything else for which thou wouldst blush if thou shouldst say that thou hadst it in thy mind. For the man who is such as no longer to delay being among the number of the best, is like a priest and minister of the gods, using too the [deity] which is planted within him, which makes the man uncontaminated by pleasure, unharmed by any pain, untouched by any insult, feeling no wrong, a fighter in the noblest fight, one who cannot be overpowered by any passion, dyed deep with justice, accepting with all his soul everything which happens and is assigned to him as his portion; and not often, nor yet without great necessity and for the general interest, imagining what another says, or does, or thinks. For it is only what belongs to himself that he makes the matter for his activity; and he constantly thinks of that which is allotted to himself out of the sum total of things, and he makes his own acts fair, and he is persuaded that his own portion is good. For the lot which is assigned to each man is carried along with him and carries him along with it.† And he remembers also that every rational animal is his kinsman, and that to care for all men is according to man's nature; and a man should hold on to the opinion not of all, but of those only who confessedly live according to nature. But as to those who live not so, he always bears in mind what kind of men they are both at home and from home, both by night and by day, and what they are, and with what men they live an impure life. Accordingly, he does not value at all the praise which comes from such men, since they are not even satisfied with themselves.

5. Labor not unwillingly, nor without regard to the common interest, nor without due consideration, nor with distraction; nor let studied ornament set off thy thoughts, and be not either a man of many words, or busy about too many things. And further, let the deity which is in thee be the guardian of a living being, manly and of ripe age, and engaged in matter political, and a Roman, and a ruler, who has taken his post like a man waiting for the signal which summons him from life, and ready to go, having need neither of oath nor of any man's testimony. Be cheerful also, and seek not external help nor the tranquillity which others give.

8

A man then must stand erect, not be kept erect by others.

6. If thou findest in human life anything better than justice, truth, temperance, fortitude, and, in a word, anything better than thy own mind's self-satisfaction in the things which it enables thee to do according to right reason, and in the condition that is assigned to thee without thy own choice; if, I say, thou seest anything better than this, turn to it with all thy soul, and enjoy that which thou hast found to be the best. But if nothing appears to be better than the deity which is planted in thee, which has subjected to itself all thy appetites, and carefully examines all the impressions, and, as Socrates said, has detached itself from the persuasions of sense, and has submitted itself to the gods, and cares for mankind; if thou findest everything else smaller and of less value than this, give place to nothing else, for if thou dost once diverge and incline to it, thou wilt no longer without distraction be able to give the preference to that good thing which is thy proper possession and thy own; for it is not right that anything of any other kind, such as praise from the many, or power, or enjoyment of pleasure, should come into competition with that which is rationally

and politically good. All these things, even though they may seem to adapt themselves [to the better things] in a small degree, obtain the superiority all at once, and carry us away. But do thou, I say, simply and freely choose the better, and hold to it — But that which is useful is the better. — Well then, if it is useful to thee as a rational being, keep to it; but if it is only useful to thee as an animal, say so, and maintain thy judgment without arrogance : only take care that thou makest the inquiry by a sure method.

7. Never value anything as profitable to thyself which shall compel thee to break thy promise, to lose thy self-respect, to hate any man, to suspect, to curse, to act the hypocrite, to desire anything which needs walls and curtains : for he who has preferred to everything else his own intelligence, and the daemon [within him] and the worship of its excellence, acts no tragic part, does not groan, will not need either solitude or much company; and, what is chief of all, he will live without either pursuing or flying from [life]; but whether for a longer or a shorter time he shall have the soul inclosed in the body, he cares not at all: for even if he must depart immediately, he will go as readily as if he were

going to do anything else which can be done with
decency and order; taking care of this only all
through life, that his thoughts turn not away
from anything which belongs to an intelligent
animal and a member of a civil community.

8. In the mind of one who is chastened and
purified thou wilt find no corrupt matter, nor im
purity, nor any sore skinned over. Nor is his
life incomplete when fate overtakes him, as one
may say of an actor who leaves the stage before ending and finishing the play. Besides,
there is in him nothing servile, nor affected, nor
too closely bound [to other things], nor yet de·
tached [from other things], nothing worthy of
blame, nothing which seeks a hiding-place.

9. Reverence the faculty which produces opinion. On this faculty it entirely depends whether
there shall exist in thy ruling part any opinion
inconsistent with nature and the constitution of
the rational animal. And this faculty promises
freedom from hasty judgment, and friendship
towards men, and obedience to the gods.

10. Throwing away then all things, hold to
these only which are few; and besides bear in
mind that every man lives only this present
time, which is an indivisible point, and that all
the rest of his life is either past or it is uncer-

tain. Short then is the time which every man
lives, and small the nook of the earth where
he lives; and short too the longest posthumous
fame, and even this only continued by a succession of poor human beings, who will very
soon die, and who know not even themselves,
much less him who died long ago.

11. To the aids which have been mentioned
let this one still be added : — Make for thyself
a definition or description of the thing which
is presented to thee, so as to see distinctly what
kind of a thing it is in its substance, in its nudity.
in its complete entirety, and tell thyself its proper
name, and the names of the things of which it
has been compounded, and into which it will be
resolved. For nothing is so productive of elevation of mind as to be able to examine methodi-
cally and truly every object which is presented
to thee in life, and always to look at things so
as to see at the same time what kind of universe
this is, and what kind of use everything performs
in it, and what value everything has with reference to the whole, and what with reference to
man, who is a citizen of the highest city, of
which all other cities are like families; what
each thing is, and of what it is composed, and
how long it is the nature of this thing to endure

which now makes an impression on me, and what
virtue I have need of with respect to it, such as
gentleness, manliness, truth, fidelity, simplicity
contentment, and the rest. Wherefore, on every
·occasion a man should say: this comes from god.
and this is according to the apportionment † and
spinning of the thread of destiny, and such-like
coincidence and chance; and this is from one
of the same stock, and a kinsman and partner,
one who knows not however what is according
to his nature. But I know; for this reason I
behave towards him according to the natural law
of fellowship with benevolence and justice. At
the same time however in things indifferent I
attempt to ascertain the value of each.

12. If thou workest at that which is before
thee, following right reason seriously, vigorously,
calmly, without allowing anything else to distract
thee, but keeping thy divine part pure, as if thou
shouldest be bound to give it back immediately;
if thou holdest to this, expecting nothing. fearing
nothing, but satisfied with thy present activity according to nature, and with heroic truth in every
word and sound which thou utterest, thou wilt
live happy. And there is no man who is able
to prevent this.

13. As physicians have always their instru-

ments and knives ready for cases which suddenly require their skill, so do thou have principles ready for the understanding of things divine and human, and for doing everything, even the smallest, with a recollection of the bond which unites the divine and human to one another. For neither wilt thou do anything well which pertains to man without at the same time having a reference to things divine ; nor the contrary.

14. No longer wander at hazard ; for neither wilt thou read thy own memoirs, nor the acts of the ancient Romans and Hellenes, and the selections from books which thou wast reserving for thy old age. Hasten then to the end which thou hast before thee, and, throwing away idle hopes, come to thy own aid, if thou carest at all for thyself, while it is in thy power.

15. They know not how many things are signified by the words stealing, sowing, buying, keeping quiet, seeing what ought to be done ; for this is not done by the eyes, but by another kind of vision.

16. Body, soul, intelligence : to the body belong sensations, to the soul appetites, to the intelligence principles. To receive the impressions of forms by means of appearances belongs even to animals ; to be pulled by the strings of

desire belongs both to wild beasts and to men
who have made themselves into women, and to a
Phalaris and a Nero: and to have the intelligence that guides to the things which appear
suitable belongs also to those who do not believe in the gods, and who betray their country,
and do their impure deeds when they have shut
the doors. If then everything else is common
to all that I have mentioned, there remains that
which is peculiar to the good man, to be pleased
and content with what happens, and with the
thread which is spun for him; and not to de-
file the divinity which is planted in his breast,
nor disturb it by a crowd of images, but to pre-
serve it tranquil, following it obediently as a god,
neither saying anything contrary to the truth, nor
doing anything contrary to justice. And if all
men refuse to believe that he lives a simple,
modest, and contented life, he is neither angry
with any of them, nor does he deviate from the
way which leads to the end of life, to which a
man ought to come pure, tranquil, ready to depart, and without any compulsion perfectly reconciled to his lot.

IV.

HAT which rules within, when it is according to nature, is so affected with respect to the events which happen, that it always easily adapts itself to that which is possible and is presented to it. For it requires no definite material, but it moves towards its purpose, under certain conditions however; and it makes a material for itself out of that which opposes it, as fire lays hold of what falls into it, by which a small light would have been extinguished: but when the fire is strong, it soon appropriates to itself the matter which is heaped on it, and consumes it, and rises higher by means of this very material.

2. Let no act be done without a purpose, nor otherwise than according to the perfect principles of art.

3. Men seek retreats for themselves, houses in

the country, sea-shores, and mountains ; and thou
too art wont to desire such things very much.
But this is altogether a mark of the most common sort of men, for it is in thy power whenever thou shalt choose to retire into thyself.
For nowhere either with more quiet or more
freedom from trouble does a man retire than
into his own soul, particularly when he has
within him such thoughts that by looking into
them he is immediately in perfect tranquillity ;
and I affirm that tranquillity is nothing else than
the good ordering of the mind.   Constantly then
give to thyself this retreat, and renew thyself;
and let thy principles be brief and fundamental,
which, as soon as thou shalt recur to them, will
be sufficient to cleanse the soul completely, and
to send thee back free from all discontent with
the things to which thou returnest.   For with
what art thou discontented ?   With the badness
of men ?   Recall to thy mind this conclusion,
that rational animals exist for one another, and
that to endure is a part of justice, and that men
do wrong involuntarily ; and consider how many
already, after mutual enmity, suspicion, hatred,
and fighting, have been stretched dead, reduced
to ashes ; and be quiet at last. — But perhaps
thou art dissatisfied with that which is assigned

to thee out of the universe. — Recall to thy recollection this alternative; either there is providence
or atoms [fortuitous concurrence of things]; or
remember the arguments by which it has been
proved that the world is a kind of political community [and be quiet at last]. — But perhaps
corporeal things will still fasten upon thee.—Consider then further that the mind mingles not with
the breath, whether moving gently or violently,
when it has once drawn itself apart and discovered its own power, and think also of all that
thou hast heard and assented to about pain and
pleasure [and be quiet at last]. — But perhaps
the desire of the thing called fame will torment
thee — See how soon everything is forgotten,
and look at the chaos of infinite time on each
side of [the present], and the emptiness of applause, and the changeableness and want of judgment in those who pretend to give praise, and
the narrowness of the space within which it is
circumscribed [and be quiet at last]. For the
whole earth is a point, and how small a nook
in it is this thy dwelling, and how few are there
in it, and what kind of people are they who will
praise thee.

This then remains : Remember to retire into
this little territory of thy own, and above all do

not distract or strain thyself, but be free, and look
at things as a man, as a human being, as a citizen,
as a mortal.   But among the things readiest to
thy hand to which thou shalt turn, let there be
these, which are two.   One is that things do not
touch the soul, for they are external and remain
immovable ; but our perturbations come only from
the opinion which is within.   The other is that
all these things which thou seest change immediately and will no longer be ; and constantly bear
in mind how many of these changes thou hast
already witnessed.   The universe is transforma-
tion : life is opinion.

4. If our intellectual part is common, the reason also, in respect of which we are rational beings, is common : if this is so, common also is the
reason which commands us what to do, and what
not to do ; if this is so, there is a common law
also ; if this is so, we are fellow-citizens ; if this
is so, we are members of some political community ; if this is so, the world is in a manner a state.
For of what other common political community
will any one say that the whole human race are
members ?   And from thence, from this common
political community comes also our very intellectual faculty and reasoning faculty and our capacity
for law ; or whence do they come ?   For as my

earthly part is a portion given to me from certain
earth, and that which is watery from another element, and that which is hot and fiery from some
peculiar source (for nothing comes out of that
which is nothing, as nothing also returns to non-
existence), so also the intellectual part comes from
some source.

5. Death is such as generation is, a mystery of
nature; a composition out of the same elements,
and a decomposition into the same; and altogether
not a thing of which any man should be ashamed,
for it is conformable to [the nature of] a reasonable animal, and not contrary to the reason of our
constitution.

6. It is natural that these things should be
done by such persons, it is a matter of necessity; and if a man will not have it so, he will
not allow the fig-tree to have juice. But by all
means bear this in mind, that within a very
short time both thou and he will be dead; and
soon not even your names will be left behind.

7. Take away thy opinion, and then there
is taken away the complaint, " I have been
harmed." Take away the complaint, " I have
been harmed," and the harm is taken away.

8. That which does not make a man worse
than he was, also does not make his life worse,

nor does it harm him either from without or
from within.

9. The nature of that which is [universally]
useful has been compelled to do this.

10. Consider that everything which happens,
happens justly, and if thou observest carefully,
thou wilt find it to be so. I do not say only
with respect to the continuity of the series of
things, but with respect to what is just, and as if
it were done by one who assigns to each thing
its value.   Observe then as thou hast begun;
and whatever thou doest, do it in conjunction
with this, the being good, and in the sense in
which a man is properly understood to be good.
Keep to this in every action.

11. Do not have such an opinion of things
as he has who does thee wrong, or such as he
wishes thee to have, but look at them as they
are in truth.

12. A man should always have these two
rules in readiness; the one, to do only whatever the reason of the ruling and legislating
faculty may suggest for the use of men; the
other, to change thy opinion, if there is any
one at hand who sets thee right and moves
thee from any opinion.   But this change of
opinion must proceed only from a certain per-

suasion, as of what is just or of common advantage, and the like, not because it appears pleasant or brings reputation.

13. Hast thou reason? I have. — Why then dost not thou use it? For if this does its own work, what else dost thou wish?

14. Thou existest as a part. Thou shalt disappear in that which produced thee; but rather thou shalt be received back into its seminal principle by transmutation.

15. Many grains of frankincense on the same altar: one falls before, another falls after; but it makes no difference.

16. Within ten days thou wilt seem a god to those to whom thou art now a beast and an ape, if thou wilt return to thy principles and the worship of reason.

17. Do not act as if thou wert going to live ten thousand years. Death hangs over thee. While thou livest, while it is in thy power, be good.

18. How much trouble he avoids who does not look to see what his neighbor says or does or thinks, but only to what he does himself, that it may be just and pure; or as Agathon † says, look not round at the depraved morals of others, but run straight along the line without deviating from it.

19. He who has a vehement desire for posthumous fame does not consider that every one of those who remember him will himself also die very soon; then again also they who have succeeded them, until the whole remembrance shall have been extinguished as it is transmitted through men who foolishly admire and perish. But suppose that those who will remember are even immortal, and that the remembrance will be immortal, what then is this to thee? And I say not what is it to the dead, but what is it to the living. What is praise, except † indeed so far as it has † a certain utility? For thou now rejectest unseasonably the gift of nature, clinging to something else . . . †.

20. Everything which is in any way beautiful is beautiful in itself, and terminates in itself, not having praise as part of itself. Neither worse then nor better is a thing made by being praised. I affirm this also of the things which are called beautiful by the vulgar, for example, material things and works of art. That which is really beautiful has no need of anything; not more than law, not more than truth, not more than benevolence or modesty. Which of these things is beautiful because it is praised, or spoiled by being blamed? Is such a thing as an emerald

made worse than it was, if it is not praised? or
gold, ivory, purple, a lyre, a little knife, a flower,
a shrub?

21. If souls continue to exist, how does the air
contain them from eternity? — But how does the
earth contain the bodies of those who have been
buried from time so remote? For as here the
mutation of these bodies after a certain continuance, whatever it may be, and their dissolution
make room for other dead bodies; so the souls
which are removed into the air after subsisting
for some time are transmuted, and diffused, and
assume a fiery nature by being received into the
seminal intelligence of the universe, and in this
way make room for the fresh souls which come
to dwell there. And this is the answer which a
man might give on the hypothesis of souls continuing to exist. But we must not only think of the
number of bodies which are thus buried, but also
of the number of animals which are daily eaten
by us and the other animals. For what a number
is consumed, and thus .in a manner buried in the
bodies of those who feed on them? And nevertheless this earth receives them by reason of the
changes [of these bodies] into blood, and the
transformations into the aërial or the fiery element.

What is the investigation into the truth in this

9

matter?   The division into that which is material
and that which is the cause of form [the formal]
(VII. 29.)

22. Do not be whirled about, but in every
movement have respect to justice, and on the oc
casion of every impression maintain the faculty
of comprehension [or understanding].

23. Everything harmonizes with me, which is
harmonious to thee, O Universe. Nothing for
me is too early nor too late, which is in due time
for thee. Everything is fruit to me which thy
seasons bring, O Nature : from thee are all things,
in thee are all things, to thee all things return.
The poet says, Dear city of Cecrops ; and wilt not
thou say, Dear city of Zeus ?

24. Occupy thyself with few things, says the
philosopher, if thou wouldst be tranquil. — But
consider if it would not be better to say, Do what
is necessary, and whatever the reason of the
animal which is naturally social requires, and as
it requires. For this brings not only the tranquillity which comes from doing well, but also that
which comes from doing few things. For the
greatest part of what we say and do being unnecessary, if a man takes this away, he will have
more leisure and less uneasiness. Accordingly
on every occasion a man should ask himself, Is

this one of the unnecessary things? Now a man should take away not only unnecessary acts, but also unnecessary thoughts, for thus superfluous acts will not follow after.

25. Try how the life of the good man suits thee, the life of him who is satisfied with his portion out of the whole, and satisfied with his own just acts and benevolent disposition.

26. Hast thou seen those things? Look also at these. Do not disturb thyself. Make thyself all simplicity. Does any one do wrong? It is to himself that he does the wrong. Has anything happened to thee? Well; out of the universe from the beginning everything which happens has been apportioned and spun out to thee. In a word, thy life is short. Thou must turn to profit the present by the aid of reason and justice. Be sober in thy relaxation.

27. Either it is a well arranged universe [1] or a chaos huddled together, but still a universe. But can a certain order subsist in thee, and disorder in the All? And this too when all things are so separated and diffused and sympathetic.

28. A black character, a womanish character,

[1] Antoninus here uses the word κόσμος both in the sense of the Universe and of Order; and it is difficult to express his meaning.

a stubborn character, bestial, childish, animal,
stupid, counterfeit, scurrilous, fraudulent, tyrannical.

29. If he is a stranger to the universe who
does not know what is in it, no less is he a
stranger who does not know what is going on
in it. He is a runaway, who flies from social
reason ; he is blind, who shuts the eyes of the
understanding ; he is poor, who has need of another, and has not from himself all things which
are useful for life. He is an abscess on the
universe who withdraws and separates himself
from the reason of our common nature through
being displeased with the things which happen,
for the same nature produces this, and has produced thee too: he is a piece rent asunder from
the state, who tears his own soul from that of
reasonable animals, which is one.

30. The one is a philosopher without a tunic,
and the other without a book : here is another
half naked :   Bread I have not, he says, and I
abide by reason — And I do not get the means
of living out of my learning,† and I abide [by
my reason].

31. Love the art, poor as it may be, which
thou hast learned, and be content with it ; and
pass through the rest of life like one who has in-

trusted to the gods with his whole soul all that he
has, making thyself neither the tyrant nor the
slave of any man.

32. Consider, for example, the times of Ves-
pasian. Thou wilt see all these things, people
marrying, bringing up children, sick, dying, war-
ring, feasting, trafficking, cultivating the ground,
flattering, obstinately arrogant, suspecting, plot-
ting, wishing for some to die, grumbling about the
present, loving, heaping up treasure, desiring con-
sulship, kingly power. Well then, that life of
these people no longer exists at all. Again, remove to the times of Trajan. Again, all is the
same. Their life too is gone. In like manner
view also the other epochs of time and of whole
nations, and see how many after great efforts soon
fell and were resolved into the elements. But
chiefly thou shouldst think of those whom thou
hast thyself known distracting themselves about
idle things, neglecting to do what was in accord-
ance with their proper constitution, and to hold
firmly to this and to be content with it. And
herein it is necessary to remember that the attention given to everything has its proper value and
proportion. For thus thou wilt not be dissatisfied,
if thou appliest thyself to smaller matters no
further than is fit.

33. The words which were formerly familiar are now antiquated: so also the names of those who were famed of old, are now in a manner antiquated, Camillus, Caeso, Volesus, Leonnatus, and a little after also Scipio and Cato, then Augustus, then also Hadrianus and Antoninus. For all things soon pass away and become a mere tale, and complete oblivion soon buries them. And I say this of those who have shone in a wondrous way. For the rest, as soon as they have breathed out their breath, they are gone, and no man speaks of them. And, to conclude the matter, what is even an eternal remembrance? A mere nothing. What then is that about which we ought to employ our serious pains? This one thing, thoughts just, and acts social, and words which never lie, and a disposition which gladly accepts all that happens, as necessary, as usual, as flowing from a principle and source of the same kind.

34. Willingly give thyself up to Clotho [one of the fates], allowing her to spin thy thread †️ into whatever things she pleases.

35. Everything is only for a day, both that which remembers and that which is remembered.

36. Observe constantly that all things take place by change, and accustom thyself to consider

that the nature of the Universe loves nothing so
much as to change the things which are and to
make new things like them. For everything that
exists is in a manner the seed of that which will
be. But thou art thinking only of seeds which
are cast into the earth or into a womb : but this
is a very vulgar notion.

37. Thou wilt soon die, and thou art not yet
simple, nor free from perturbations, nor without
suspicion of being hurt by external things, nor
kindly disposed towards all; nor dost thou yet
place wisdom only in acting justly.

38. Examine men's ruling principles, even
those of the wise, what kind of things they avoid,
and what kind they pursue.

39. What is evil to thee does not subsist in
the ruling principle of another; nor yet in any
turning and mutation of thy corporeal covering.
Where is it then? It is in that part of thee in
which subsists the power of forming opinions
about evils. Let this power then not form [such]
opinions, and all is well. And if that which is
nearest to it, the poor body, is cut, burnt, filled
with matter and rottenness, nevertheless let the
part which forms opinions about these things be
quiet, that is, let it judge that nothing is either
bad or good which can happen equally to the bad

man and the good. For that which happens
equally to him who. lives contrary to nature and
to him who lives according to nature, is neither
according to nature nor contrary to nature.

40. Constantly regard the universe as one living being, having one substance and one soul;
and observe how all things have reference to one
perception, the perception of this one living being;
and how all things act with one movement; and
how all things are the co-operating causes of all
things which exist; observe too the continuous
spinning of the thread and the contexture of the
web.

41. Thou art a little soul bearing about a
corpse, as Epictetus used to say.

42. It is no evil for things to undergo change,
and no good for things to subsist in consequence
of change.

43. Time is like a river made up of the events
which happen, and a violent stream; for as soon
as a thing has been seen, it is carried away, and
another comes in its place, and this will be carried away too.

44. Everything which happens is as familiar
and well known as the rose in spring and the
fruit in summer; for such is disease, and death,
and calumny, and treachery, and whatever else
delights fools or vexes them.

45. In the series of things those which follow are always aptly fitted to those which have gone before ; for this series is not like a mere enumeration of disjointed things, which has only a necessary sequence, but it is a rational connection: and as all existing things are arranged together harmoniously, so the things which come into existence exhibit no mere succession, but a certain wonderful relationship. (vi. 38. vii. 9.)

46. Always remember the saying of Heraclitus, that the death of earth is to become water, and the death of water is to become air, and the death of air is to become fire, and reversely. And think too of him who forgets whither the way leads, and that men quarrel with that with which they are most constantly in communion, the reason which governs the universe ; and the things which they daily meet with seem to them strange : and consider that we ought not to act and speak as if we were asleep, for even in sleep we seem to act and speak ; and that † we ought not, like children who learn from their parents, simply to act and speak as we have been taught.†

47. If any god told thee that thou shalt die to-morrow or certainly on the day after to-morrow, thou wouldst not care much whether it was on the third day or on the morrow, unless thou wast in

the highest degree mean-spirited, — for how small is the difference? — so think it no great thing to die after as many years as thou canst name rather than to-morrow.

48. Think continually how many physicians are dead after often contracting their eyebrows over the sick; and how many astrologers after predicting with great pretensions the deaths of others; and how many philosophers after endless discourses on death or immortality; how many heroes after killing thousands; and how many tyrants who have used their power over men's lives with terrible insolence as if they were immortal; and how many cities are entirely dead, so to speak, Helice and Pompeii and Herclanum, and others innumerable. Add to the reckoning all whom thou hast known, one after another. One man after burying another has been laid out dead, and another buries him; and all this in a short time. To conclude, always observe how ephemeral an worthless human things are, and what was yesterday a little mucus, to-morrow will be a mummy or ashes. Pass then through this little space of time conformably to nature, and end thy journey in content, just as an olive falls off when it is ripe, blessing nature who produced it, and thanking the tree on which it grew.

49. Be like the promontory against which the waves continually break, but it stands firm and tames the fury of the water around it.

Unhappy am I, because this has happened to me — Not so, but Happy am I, though this has happened to me, because I continue free from pain, neither crushed by the present nor fearing the future. For such a thing as this might have happened to every man : but every man would not have continued free from pain on such an occasion. Why then is that rather a misfortune than this a good fortune? And dost thou in all cases call that a man's misfortune, which is not a deviation from man's nature? And does a thing seem to thee to be a deviation from man's nature, when it is not contrary to the will of man's nature? Well, thou knowest the will of nature. Will then this which has happened prevent thee from being just, magnanimous, temperate, prudent, secure against inconsiderate opinions and falsehood; will it prevent thee from having modesty, freedom, and everything else, by the presence of which man's nature obtains all that is its own? Remember too on every occasion which leads thee to vexation to apply this principle: that this is not a misfortune, but that to bear it nobly is good fortune.

50. It is a vulgar, but still a useful help towards contempt of death, to pass in review those who have tenaciously stuck to life. What more then have they gained than those who have died early? Certainly they lie in their tombs somewhere at last, Cadicianus, Fabius, Julianus, Lepidus, or any one else like them, who have carried out many to be buried and then were carried out themselves. Altogether the interval is small [between birth and death]; and consider with how much trouble, and in company with what sort of people and in what a feeble body this interval is laboriously passed. Do not then consider life a thing of any value.† For look to the immensity of time behind thee, and to the time which is before thee, another boundless space. In this infinity then what is the difference between him who lives three days and him who lives three generations? ²

51. Always run to the short way; and the short

² An allusion to Homer's Nestor who was living at the war of Troy among the third generation, like old Parr with his hundred and fifty two years, and some others in modern times who have beaten Parr by twenty or thirty years; and yet they died at last. The word is τριγερηνίου in Antoninus. Nestor is named τριγέρων by some writers; but here perhaps there is an allusion to Homer's Γερήνιος ἱππότα Νέστωρ.

way is the natural : accordingly say and do everything in conformity with the soundest reason.
For such a purpose frees a man from trouble,†
and warfare, and all artifice and ostentatious
display.

V.

IN the morning when thou risest unwillingly, let this thought be present — I am rising to the work of a human being. Why then am I dissatisfied if I am going to do the things for which I exist and for which I was brought into the world? Or have I been made for this, to lie in the bedclothes and keep myself warm? — But this is more pleasant — Dost thou exist then to take thy pleasure. and not at all for action or exertion? Dost thou not see the little plants, the little birds, the ants, the spiders, the bees working together to put in order their several parts of the universe? And art thou unwilling to do the work of a human being, and dost thou not make haste to do that which is according to thy nature? — But it is necessary to take rest also — It is necessary: however nature has fixed bounds to this too: she has fixed bounds both to eating and

drinking, and yet thou goest beyond these bounds,
beyond what is sufficient; yet in thy acts it is not
so, but thou stoppest short of what thou canst do.
So thou lovest not thyself, for if thou didst, thou
wouldst love thy nature and her will. But those
who love their several arts exhaust themselves in
working at them, unwashed and without food ; but
thou valuest thy own nature less than the turner
values the turning art, or the dancer the dancing
art, or the lover of money values his money, or
the vainglorious man his little glory. And such
men, when they have a violent affection to a thing,
choose neither to eat nor to sleep rather than to
perfect the things which they care for. But are
the acts which concern society more vile in thy
eyes and less worthy of thy labor?

2. How easy it is to repel and to wipe away
every impression which is troublesome or unsuit-
able, and immediately to be in all tranquillity.

3. Judge every word and deed which is according to nature to be fit for thee ; and be not diverted
by the blame which follows from any people nor
by their words, but if a thing is good to be done
or said, do not consider it unworthy of thee. For
those persons have their peculiar leading principle
and follow their peculiar movement; which things
do not thou regard, but go straight on, following

thy own nature and the common nature; and the way of both is one.

4. I go through the things which happen according to nature until I shall fall and rest, breathing out my breath into that element out of which I daily draw it in, and falling upon that earth out of which my father collected the, seed, and my mother the blood, and my nurse the milk; out of which during so many years I have been supplied with food and drink; which bears me when I tread on it and abuse it for so many purposes.

5. Thou sayest, Men cannot admire the sharpness of thy wits — Be it so; but there are many other things of which thou canst not say, I am not formed for them by nature. Show those qualities then which are altogether in thy power, sincerity, gravity, endurance of labor, aversion to pleasure, contentment with thy portion and with few things, benevolence, frankness, no love of superfluity, freedom from trifling, magnanimity. Dost thou not see how many qualities thou art immediately able to exhibit, in which there is no excuse of natural incapacity and unfitness, and yet thou still remainest voluntarily below the mark? or art thou compelled through being defectively furnished by nature to murmur, and to be stingy, and to flatter,

and to find fault with thy poor body, and to try
to please men, and to make great display, and to
be so restless in thy mind? No by the gods: but
thou mightest have been delivered from these
things long ago. Only if in truth thou canst be
charged with being rather slow and dull of comprehension, thou must exert thyself about this
also, not neglecting it nor yet taking pleasure in
thy dulness.

6. One man, when he has done a service to
another, is ready to set it down to his account as
a favor conferred. Another is not ready to do
this, but still in his own mind he thinks of the
man as his debtor, and he knows what he has
done. A third in a manner does not even know ·
what he has done, but he is like a vine which has
produced grapes, and seeks for nothing more after
it has once produced its proper fruit. As a horse
when he has run, a dog when he has tracked the
game, a bee when it has made the honey, so a man
when he has done a good act, does not call out for
others to come and see, but he goes on to another
act, as a vine goes on to produce again the grapes
in season — Must a man then be one of these,
who in a manner act thus without observing it? —
Yes — But this very thing is necessary, the observation of what a man is doing: for, it may be

10

said, it is characteristic of the social animal to
perceive that he is working in a social manner,
and indeed to wish that his social partner also
should perceive it — It is true what thou sayest,
but thou dost not rightly understand what is now
said : and for this reason thou wilt become one of
those of whom I spoke before, for even they are
misled by a certain show of reason. But if thou
wilt choose to understand the meaning of what is
said, do not fear that for this reason thou wilt
omit any social act.

7. A prayer of the Athenians : Rain, rain, O
dear Zeus, down on the ploughed fields of the
Athenians and on the plains. — In truth we ought
not to pray at all, or we ought to pray in this simple and noble fashion.

8. Just as we must understand when it is said,
That Aesculapius prescribed to this man horse-
exercise, or bathing in cold water or going without shoes; so we must understand it when it is
said, That the nature of the universe prescribed
to this man disease or mutilation or loss or anything else of the kind. For in the first case Prescribed means something like this : he prescribed
this for this man as a thing adapted to procure
health ; and in the second case it means, That

which happens [1] to [or, suits] every man is fixed
in a manner for him suitably to his destiny. For
this is what we mean when we say that things are
suitable to us, as the workmen say of squared
stones in walls or the pyramids, that they are
suitable, when they fit them to one another in
some kind of connection. For there is altogether
one fitness [or, harmony]. And as the universe
is made up out of all bodies to be such a body as
it is, so out of all existing causes necessity [des-
tiny] is made up to be such a cause as it is. And
even those who are completely ignorant understand what I mean, for they say, It [necessity,
destiny] brought this to such a person. — This
then was brought and this was prescribed to
him. Let us then receive these things, as well as
those which Aesculapius prescribes. Many as a
matter of course even among his prescriptions are
disagreeable, but we accept them in the hope of
health. Let the perfecting and accomplishment
of the things which the common nature judges to
be good, be judged by thee to be of the same kind
as thy health. And so accept everything which
happens, even if it seem disagreeable, because it
leads to this, to the health of the universe and to

[1] In this section there is a play on the meaning of
συμβαίνειν.

the prosperity and felicity of Zeus [the universe].
For he would not have brought on any man what
he has brought, if it were not useful for the
whole.   Neither does the nature of anything,
whatever it may be, cause anything which is not
suitable to that which is directed by it.   For two
reasons then it is right to be content with that
which happens to thee; the one, because it was
done for thee and prescribed for thee, and in a
manner had reference to thee, originally from the
most ancient causes spun with thy destiny; and
the other, because even that which comes severally to every man is to the power which administers the universe a cause of felicity and perfection,
nay even of its very continuance.   For the in-
tegrity of the whole is mutilated, if thou cuttest
off anything whatever from the conjunction and
the continuity either of the parts or of the causes.
And thou dost cut off, as far as it is in thy power,
when thou art dissatisfied, and in a manner triest
to put anything out of the way.

9. Be not disgusted, nor discouraged, nor dissatisfied, if thou dost not succeed in doing everything according to right principles; but when thou
hast failed, return back again, and be content if
the greater part of what thou doest is consistent
with man's nature, and love this to which thou re-

turnest; and do not return to philosophy as if she
were a master, but act like those who have sore
eyes and apply a bit of sponge and egg, or as
another applies a plaister, or drenching with water.
For thus thou wilt not fail to † obey reason, and
thou wilt repose in it. And remember that philosophy requires only the things which thy nature
requires; but thou wouldst have something else
which is not according to nature — It may be ob-
jected, Why what is more agreeable than this
[which I am doing]? — But is not this the very
reason why pleasure deceives us? And consider
if magnanimity, freedom, simplicity, aequanimity,
piety, are not more agreeable. For what is more
agreeable than wisdom itself, when thou thinkest
of the security and the happy course of all things
which depend on the faculty of understanding
and knowledge?

10. Things are in such a kind of envelopement
that they have seemed to philosophers, not a few
nor those common philosophers, altogether unintelligible; nay even to the Stoics themselves they
seem difficult to understand. And all our assent
is changeable; for where is the man who never
changes? Carry thy thoughts then to the objects
themselves, and consider how short-lived they are
and worthless, and that they may be in the pos-

session of a filthy wretch or a whore or a robber
Then turn to the morals of those who live with
thee, and it is hardly possible to endure even the
most agreeable of them, to say nothing of a man
being hardly able to endure himself. In such
darkness then and dirt and in so constant a flux
both of substance and of time, and of motion and
of things moved, what there is worth being highly
prized or even an object of serious pursuit, I cannot imagine. But on the contrary it is a man's
duty to comfort himself, and to wait for the
natural dissolution and not to be vexed at the
delay, but to rest in these principles only : the one,
that nothing will happen to me which is not conformable to the nature of the universe ; and the
other, that it is in my power never to act contrary
to my god and daemon : for there is no man who
will compel me to this.

11. About what am I now employing my own
soul ? On every occasion I must ask myself this
question, and inquire, what have I now in this
part of me which they call the ruling principle ?
and whose soul have I now ? that of a child, or of
a young man, or of a feeble woman, or of a tyrant,
or of a domestic animal, or of a wild beast ?

12. What kind of things those are which appear good to the many, we may learn from this.

For if any man should conceive certain things as being really good, such as prudence, temperance, justice, fortitude, he would not after having first conceived these endure to listen to anything †which should not be in harmony with what is really good.† But if a man has first conceived as good the things which appear to the many to be good, he will listen and readily receive as very applicable that which was said by the comic writer. † Thus even the many perceive the difference.† For were it not so, this saying would not offend and would not be rejected [in the first case], while we receive it when it is said of wealth, and of the means which further luxury and fame, as said fitly and wittily. Go on then and ask if we should value and think those things to be good, to which after their first conception in the mind the words of the comic writer might be aptly applied — that he who has them, through pure abundance has not a place to ease himself in.

13. I am composed of the formal and the material; and neither of them will perish into non-existence, as neither of them came into existence out of non-existence. Every part of me then will be reduced by change into some part of the universe, and that again will change into another part of the universe and so on for ever. And by

consequence of such a change I too exist, and those who begot me, and so on for ever in the other direction. For nothing hinders us from saying so, even if the universe is administered according to definite periods [of revolution].

14. Reason and the reasoning art [philosophy] are powers which are sufficient for themselves and for their own works. They move then from a first principle which is their own, and they make their way to the end which is proposed to them ; and this is the reason why such acts are named Catorthóseis or right acts, which word signifies that they proceed by the right road.

15. None of these things ought to be called a man's, which do not belong to a man, as man. They are not required of a man, nor does man's nature promise them, nor are they the means of man's nature attaining its end. Neither then does the end of man lie in these things, nor yet that which aids to the accomplishment of this end, and that which aids towards this end is that which is good. Besides, if any of these things did belong to man, it would not be right for a man to despise them and to set himself against them ; nor would a man be worthy of praise who showed that he did not want these things, nor would he who stinted himself in any of them be

good, if indeed these things were good. But now
the more of these things a man deprives himself
of, or of other things like them, or even when he
is deprived of any of them, the more patiently
he endures the loss, just in the same degree he is
a better man.

16. Such as are thy habitual thoughts, such
also will be the character of thy mind; for the
soul is dyed by the thoughts. Dye it then with a
continuous series of such thoughts as these : for
instance, that where a man can live, there he can
also live well. But he must live in a palace ;
— well then, he can also live well in a palace.
And again, consider that for whatever purpose
each thing has been constituted, for this it has
been constituted, and towards this it is carried ;
and its end is in that towards which it is carried ;
and where the end is, there also is the advantage
and the good of each thing. Now the good for
the reasonable animal is society ; for that we are
made for society has been shown above. Is it not
plain that the inferior exist for the sake of the
superior? but the things which have life are
superior to those which have not life, and of those
which have life the superior are those which have
reason.

17. To seek what is impossible is madness:

and it is impossible that the bad should not do something of this kind.

18. Nothing happens to any man which he is not formed by nature to bear. The same things happen to another, and either because he does not see that they have happened or because he would show a great spirit he is firm and remains unharmed. It is a shame then that ignorance and conceit should be stronger than wisdom.

19. Things themselves touch not the soul, not in the least degree; nor have they admission to the soul, nor can they turn or move the soul: but the soul turns and moves itself alone, and whatever judgments it may think proper to make, such it makes for itself the things which present themselves to it.

20. In one respect man is the nearest thing to me, so far as I must do good to men and endure them. But so far as some men make themselves obstacles to my proper acts, man becomes to me one of the things which are indifferent, no less than the sun or wind or a wild beast. Now it is true that these may impede my action, but they are no impediments to my affects and disposition, which have the power of acting conditionally and changing: for the mind converts and changes every hindrance to its activity into an aid; and so

that which is a hindrance is made a furtherance
to an act; and that which is an obstacle on the
road helps us on this road.

21. Reverence that which is best in the universe; and this is that which makes use of all
things and directs all things. And in like manner
also reverence that which is best in thyself; and
this is of the same kind as that. For in thyself
also, that which makes use of everything else, is
this, and thy life is directed by this.

22. That which does no harm to the state, does
no harm to the citizen. In the case of every appearance of harm apply this rule: if the state is
not harmed by this, neither am I harmed. But
if the state is harmed, thou must not be angry
with him who does harm to the state. Show him
where his error is.†

23. Often think of the rapidity with which
things pass by and disappear, both the things
which are and the things which are produced.
For substance is like a river in a continual flow,
and the activities of things are in constant change,
and the causes work in infinite varieties; and
there is hardly anything which stands still. And
consider this which is near to thee, this boundless
abyss of the past and of the future in which all
things disappear. How then is he not a fool who

is puffed up with such things or plagued about them and makes himself miserable? for they vex him only for a time, and a short time.

24. Think of the universal substance, of which thou hast a very small portion; and of universal time, of which a short and indivisible interval has been assigned to thee; and of that which is fixed by destiny, and how small a part of it thou art.

25. Does another do me wrong? Let him look to it. He has his own disposition, his own activity. I now have what the universal nature wills me to have; and I do what my nature now wills me to do.

26. Let the part of thy soul which leads and governs be undisturbed by the movements in the flesh whether of pleasure or of pain; and let it not unite with them, but let it circumscribe itself and limit those affects to their parts. But when these affects rise up to the mind by virtue of that other sympathy that naturally exists in a body which is all one, then thou must not strive to resist the sensation, for it is natural; but let not the ruling part of itself add to the sensation the opinion that it is either good or bad.

27. Live with the gods. And he does live with the gods who constantly shows to them that his own soul is satisfied with that which is assigned to

him, and that it does all that the daemon wishes, which Zeus hath given to every man for his guardian and guide, a portion of himself. And this is every man's understanding and reason.

28. Art thou angry with him whose arm-pits stink? art thou angry with him whose mouth smells foul? What good will this anger do thee? He has such a mouth, he has such arm-pits: it is necessary that such an emanation must come from such things — But the man has reason, it will be said, and he is able, if he takes pains, to discover wherein he offends — I wish thee well of thy discovery. Well then, and thou hast reason : by thy rational faculty stir up his rational faculty; show him his error, admonish him. For if he listens, thou wilt cure him, and there is no need of anger. [† Neither tragic actor nor whore.†]²

29. As thou intendest to live when thou art gone out, . . so it is in thy power to live here. But if men do not permit thee, then get away out

---

² This is imperfect or corrupt, or both. There is also something wrong or incomplete in the beginning of S. 29, where he says ὡς ἐξελθὼν ζῆν διανοῇ, which Gataker translates "as if thou wast about to quit life;" but we cannot translate ἐξελθὼν in that way. Other translations are not much more satisfactory. I have translated it literally and left it imperfect.

of life, yet so as if thou wert suffering no harm.
The house is smoky, and I quit it. Why dost
thou think that this is any trouble? But so long
as nothing of the kind drives me out, I remain,
am free, and no man shall hinder me from doing
what I choose; and I choose to do what is according to the nature of the rational and social
animal.

30. The intelligence of the universe is social.
Accordingly it has made the inferior things for
the sake of the superior, and it has fitted the superior to one another. Thou seest how it has
subordinated, co-ordinated and assigned to everything its proper portion, and has brought together
into concord with one another the things which
are the best.

31. How hast thou behaved hitherto to the
gods, thy parents, brethren, children, teachers, to
those who looked after thy infancy, to thy friends,
kinsfolk, to thy slaves? Consider if thou hast
hitherto behaved to all in such a way that this
may be said of thee : —

Never has wronged a man in deed or word.

And call to recollection both how many things
thou hast passed through, and how many things
thou hast been able to endure : and that the his-

tory of thy life is now complete and thy service is ended: and how many beautiful things thou hast seen : and how many pleasures and pains thou hast despised; and how many things called honorable thou hast spurned ; and to how many ill-minded folks thou hast shown a kind disposition.

32. Why do unskilled and ignorant souls disturb him who has skill and knowledge ? What soul then has skill and knowledge ? That which knows beginning and end, and knows the reason which pervades all substance and through all time by fixed periods [revolutions] administers the universe.

33. Soon, very soon, thou wilt be ashes, or a skeleton, and either a name or not even a name ; but name is sound and echo. And the things which are much valued in life are empty and rotten and trifling, and [like] little dogs biting one another, and little children quarrelling, laughing, and then straightway weeping. But fidelity and modesty and justice and truth are fled

> Up to Olympus from the wide-spread earth.

What then is there which still detains thee here ? if the objects of sense are easily changed and never stand still, and the organs of perception are

dull and easily receive false impressions ; and the
poor soul itself is an exhalation from blood.   But
to have good repute amidst such a world as this
is an empty thing.   Why then dost thou not wait
in tranquillity for thy end, whether it is extinction
or removal to another state?   And until that time
comes, what is sufficient?   Why, what else than
to venerate the gods and bless them, and to do
good to men, and to practise tolerance and self-
restraint ; [3] but as to everything which is beyond
the limits of the poor flesh and breath, to remember that this is neither thine nor in thy power.

34.   Thou canst pass thy life in an equable flow
of happiness, if thou canst go by the right way,
and think and act in the right way.   These two
things are common both to the soul of god and to
the soul of man, and to the soul of every rational
being, not to be hindered by another ; and to hold
good to consist in the disposition to justice and the
practice of it, and in this to let thy desire find its
termination.

35.   If this is neither my own badness, nor an
effect of my own badness, and the common weal is

---

[3] This is the Stoic precept ἀνέχου καὶ ἀπέχου.   The
first part teaches us to be content with men and things
as they are.   The second part teaches us the virtue of
self-restraint, or the government of our passions.

not injured, why am I troubled about it? and what is the harm to the common weal?

36. Do not be carried along inconsiderately by the appearance of things, but give help [to all] according to thy ability and their fitness; and if they should have sustained loss in matters which are indifferent, do not imagine this to be a damage. For it is a bad habit. But as the old man when he went away asked back his foster-child's top, remembering that it was a top, so do thou in this case also.

When thou art calling out on the Rostra, hast thou forgotten, man, what these things are? — Yes; but they are objects of great concern to these people — Wilt thou too then be made a fool for these things? — I was once a fortunate man, but I lost it, I know not how. — But fortunate means that a man has assigned to himself a good fortune: — and a good fortune is good disposition of the soul, good emotions, good actions.[4]

[4] This section is unintelligible. Many of the words may be corrupt, and the general purport of the section cannot be discovered. Perhaps several things have been improperly joined in one section. I have translated it nearly literally. Different translators give the section a different turn, and the critics have tried to mend what they cannot understand.

11

VI.

THE substance of the universe is obedient and compliant; and the reason which governs it has in itself no cause for doing evil, for it has no malice, nor does it do evil to anything, nor is anything harmed by it. But all things are made and perfected according to this reason.

2. Let it make no difference to thee whether thou art cold or warm, if thou art doing thy duty; and whether thou art drowsy or satisfied with sleep; and whether ill-spoken of or praised; and whether dying or doing something else. For it is one of the acts of life, this act by which we die: it is sufficient then in this act also to do well what we have in hand.

3. Look within. Let neither the peculiar quality of anything nor its value escape thee.

4. All existing things soon change, and they will either be reduced to vapor, if indeed all substance is one, or they will be dispersed.

5. The reason which governs knows what its own disposition is, and what it does, and on what material it works.

6. The best way of avenging thyself is not to become like the wrong doer.

7. Take pleasure in one thing and rest in it, in passing from one social act to another social act, thinking of god.

8. The ruling principle is that which rouses and turns itself, and while it makes itself such as it is and such as it wills to be, it also makes everything which happens appear to itself to be such as it wills.

9. In conformity to the nature of the universe every single thing is accomplished, for certainly it is not in conformity to any other nature that each thing is accomplished, either a nature which externally comprehends this, or a nature which is comprehended within this nature, or a nature external and independent of this. (XI. 1, VI. 40, VIII. 50.)

10. The universe is either a confusion, and a mutual involution of things, and a dispersion ; or it is unity and order and providence. If then it is the former, why do I desire to tarry in a fortuitous combination of things and such a disorder? and why do I care about anything else than how I

shall at last become earth? and why am I disturbed, for the dispersion of my elements will
happen whatever I do. But if the other supposition is true, I venerate, and I am firm, and I trust
in him who governs. (IV. 27.)

11. When thou hast been compelled by circumstances to be disturbed in a manner, quickly
return to thyself and do not continue out of tune
longer than the compulsion lasts; for thou wilt
have more mastery over the harmony by continually recurring to it.

12. If thou hadst a step-mother and a mother
at the same time, thou wouldst be dutiful to thy
step-mother, but still thou wouldst constantly return to thy mother. Let the court and philosophy
now be to thee step-mother and mother: return
to philosophy frequently and repose in her, through
whom what thou meetest with in the court appears
to thee tolerable, and thou appearest tolerable in
the court.

13. When we have meat before us and such
eatables, we receive the impression, that this is
the dead body of a fish, and this is the dead body
of a bird or of a pig; and again, that this Faler-
nian is only a little grape juice, and this purple
robe some sheeps' wool dyed with the blood of a
shell-fish: such then are these impressions, and

they reach the things themselves and penetrate
them, and so we see what kind of things they are.
Just in the same way ought we to act all through
life, and where there are things which appear
most worthy of our approbation, we ought to lay
them bare and look at their worthlessness and
strip them of all the words by which they are
exalted. For outward show is a wonderful per-
verter of the reason, and when thou art most sure
that thou art employed about things worth thy
pains, it is then that it cheats thee most. Consider then what Crates says of Xenocrates himself.

14. Most of the things which the multitude
admire are referred to objects of the most general
kind, those which are held together by cohesion
or natural organization, such as stones, wood, fig-
trees, vines, olives. But those which are admired
by men, who are a little more reasonable, are referred to the things which are held together by a
living principle, as flocks, herds. Those which
are admired by men who are still more instructed
are the things which are held together by a rational soul, not however a universal soul, but rational so far as it is a soul skilled in some art, or
expert in some other way, or simply rational so
far as the possessing of a number of slaves. But
he who values a rational soul, a soul universal and

fitted for political life, regards nothing else except
this; and above all things he keeps his soul in a
condition and in an activity conformable to reason
and social life, and he co-operates to this end with
those who are of the same kind as himself.

15. Some things are hurrying into existence,
and others are hurrying out of it; and of that
which is coming into existence part is already extinguished. Motions and changes are continually
renewing the world, just as the uninterrupted
course of time is always renewing the infinite duration of ages. In this flowing stream then, on
which there is no abiding, what is there of the
things which hurry by on which a man would set
a high price? It would be just as if a man should
fall in love with one of the sparrows which fly by,
but it has already past out of sight. Something
of this kind is the very life of every man, like the
exhalation of the blood and the respiration of the
air. For such as it is to have once drawn in the
air and to have given it back, which we do every
moment, just the same is it with the whole respi-
ratory power, which thou didst receive at thy birth
yesterday and the day before, to give it back to
the element from which thou didst first draw it.

16. Neither is transpiration, as in plants, a
thing to be valued, nor respiration, as in domesti-

cated animals and wild beasts, nor the receiving
of impressions by the appearances of things, nor
being moved by desires as puppets by strings, nor
assembling in herds, nor being nourished by food;
for this is just like the act of separating and part-
ing with the useless part of our food. What then
is worth being valued? To be received with
clapping of hands? No. Neither must we value
the clapping of tongues, for the praise which
comes from the many is a clapping of tongues.
Suppose then that thou hast given up this worthless thing called fame, what remains that is worth
valuing? This in my opinion, to move thyself
and to restrain thyself in conformity to thy proper
constitution, to which end all employments lead
and all arts. For every art aims at this, that the
thing which has been made should be adapted to
the work for which it has been made; and both
the vine-planter who looks after the vine, and the
horse-breaker, and he who trains the dog, seek
this end. But the education and the teaching of
youth aim at something. In this then is the
value of the education and the teaching. And if
this is well, thou wilt not seek anything else.
Wilt thou not cease to value many other things
too? Then thou wilt be neither free, nor sufficient for thy own happiness, nor without passion.

For of necessity thou must be envious, jealous,
and suspicious of those who can take away those
things, and plot against those who have that
which is valued by thee. Of necessity a man
must be altogether in a state of perturbation who
wants any of these things: and besides, he must
often find fault with the gods. But to reverence
and honor thy own mind will make thee content
with thyself, and in harmony with society, and in
agreement with the gods, that is, praising all that
they give and have ordered.

17. Above, below, all around are the movements
of the elements. But the motion of virtue is in
none of these: it is something more divine, and
advancing by a way hardly observed it goes happily on its road.

18. How strangely men act. They will not
praise those who are living at the same time and
living with themselves; but to be themselves
praised by posterity, by those whom they have
never seen nor ever will see, this they set much
value on. But this is very much the same as if
thou shouldst be grieved because those who have
lived before thee did not praise thee.

19. If a thing is difficult to be accomplished by
thyself, do not think that it is impossible for a
man: but if anything is possible for a man and

conformable to his nature, think that this can be attained by thyself too.

20. In the gymnastic exercises suppose that a man has torn thee with his nails, and by dashing against thy head has inflicted a wound. Well, we neither show any signs of vexation, nor are we offended, nor do we suspect him afterwards as a treacherous fellow; and yet we are on our guard against him, not however as an enemy, nor yet with suspicion, but we quietly get out of his way. Something like this let thy behavior be in all the other parts of life; let us overlook many things in those who are like antagonists in the gymnasium. For it is in our power, as I said, to get out of the way, and to have no suspicion nor hatred.

21. If any man is able to convince me and show me that I do not think or act right, I will gladly change; for I seek the truth by which no man was ever injured. But he is injured who abides in his error and ignorance.

22. I do my duty: other things trouble me not; for they are either things without life, or things without reason, or things that have rambled and know not the way.

23. As to the animals which have no reason and generally all things and objects do thou, since thou hast reason and they have none, make use

of them with a generous and liberal spirit. But towards human beings, as they have reason, behave in a social spirit. And on all occasions call on the gods, and do not perplex thyself about the length of time in which thou shalt do this; for even three hours so spent are sufficient.

24. Alexander the Macedonian and his groom by death were brought to the same state; for either they were received among the same seminal principles of the universe, or they were alike dispersed among the atoms.

25. Consider how many things in the same indivisible time take place in each of us, things which concern the body and things which concern the soul: and so thou wilt not wonder if many more things, or rather all things which come into existence in that which is the one and all, which we call Cosmos, exist in it at the same time.

26. If any man should propose to thee the question, how the name Antoninus is written, wouldst thou with a straining of the voice utter each letter? What then if they grow angry, wilt thou be angry too? Wilt thou not go on with composure and number every letter? Just so then in this life also remember that every duty is made up of certain parts. These it is thy duty to observe, and without being disturbed or show-

ing anger towards those who are angry with thee to go on thy way and finish that which is set before thee.

27. How cruel it is not to allow men to strive after the things which appear to them to be suitable to their nature and profitable! And yet in a manner thou dost not allow them to do this, when thou art vexed because they do wrong. For they are certainly moved towards things because they suppose them to be suitable to their nature and profitable to them — But it is not so — Teach them then, and show them without being angry.

28. Death is a cessation of the impressions through the senses, and of the pulling of the strings which move the appetites, and of the discursive movements of the thoughts, and of the service to the flesh.

29. It is a shame for the soul to be first to give way in this life, when thy body does not give way.

30. Take care that thou art not made into a Caesar, that thou art not dyed with this dye ; for such things happen. Keep thyself then simple, good, pure, serious, free from affectation, a friend of justice, a worshipper of the gods, kind, affectionate, strenuous in all proper acts. Strive to

continue to be such as philosophy wished to make
thee. Reverence the gods, and help men. Short
is life. There is only one fruit of this terrene
life, a pious disposition and social acts. Do
everything as a disciple of Antoninus. Remember his constancy in every act which was conformable to reason, and his evenness in all things,
and his piety, and the serenity of his countenance,
and his sweetness, and his disregard of empty
fame, and his efforts to understand things; and
how he would never let anything pass without
having first most carefully examined it and clearly
understood it; and how he bore with those who
blamed him unjustly without blaming them in return; how he did nothing in a hurry; and how he
listened not to calumnies, and how exact an exam-
iner of manners and actions he was; and not given
to reproach people, nor timid, nor suspicious, nor
a sophist; and with how little he was satisfied,
such as lodging, bed, dress, food, servants; and
how laborious and patient; and how he was able
on account of his sparing diet to hold out to the
evening, not even requiring to relieve himself by
any evacuations except at the usual hour; and
his firmness and uniformity in his friendships;
and how he tolerated freedom of speech in those
who opposed his opinions; and the pleasure **that**

he had when any man showed him anything better; and how pious he was without superstition.
Imitate all this that thou mayest have as good a
conscience, when thy last hour comes, as he had.
(I. 16.)

31. Return to thy sober senses and call thyself
back; and when thou hast roused thyself from
sleep and hast perceived that they were only
dreams which troubled thee, now in thy waking
hours look at these [the things about thee] as
thou didst look at those [the dreams].

32. I consist of a little body and a soul. Now
to this little body all things are indifferent, for it
is not able to perceive differences. But to the
understanding those things only are indifferent,
which are not the works of its own activity. But
whatever things are the works of its own activity,
all these are in its power. And of these however only those which are done with reference to
the present; for as to the future and the past
activities of the mind, even these are for the
present indifferent.

33. Neither the labor which the hand does nor
that of the foot is contrary to nature, so long as
the foot does the foot's work and the hand the
hand's. So then neither to a man as a man is his
labor contrary to nature, so long as it does the

things of a man. But if the labor is not contrary
to his nature, neither is it an evil to him.

34. How many pleasures have been enjoyed
by robbers, patricides, tyrants.

35. Dost thou not see how the handicraftsmen
accommodate themselves up to a certain point to
those who are not skilled in their craft, — nevertheless they cling to the reason [the principles]
of their art and do not endure to depart from it?
Is it not strange if the architect and the physician
shall have more respect to the reason [the prin-
ciples] of their own arts than man to his own
reason, which is common to him and the gods.

36. Asia, Europe are corners of the universe :
all the sea a drop in the universe ; Athos a little
clod of the universe : all the present time is a
point in eternity. All things are little, changeable, perishable. All things come from thence,
from that universal ruling power either directly
proceeding or by way of consequence. And accordingly the lion's gaping jaws, and that which
is poisonous, and every harmful thing, as a thorn,
as mud, are after-products of the grand and beautiful. Do not then imagine that they are of another kind from that which thou dost venerate,
but form a just opinion of the source of all.

37. He who has seen present things has seen

all, both everything which has taken place from
all eternity and everything which will be for time
without end; for all are of one kin and of one
form.

38. Frequently consider the connection of all
things in the universe and their relation to one
another. For in a manner all things are implicated with one another, and all in this way are
friendly to one another; for one thing comes in
order after another, and this is by virtue of the†
active movement and mutual conspiration and the
unity of the substance.

39. Adapt thyself to the things with which thy
lot has been cast: and the men among whom
thou hast received thy portion, love them, but do
it truly [sincerely].

40. Every instrument, tool, vessel, if it does
that for which it has been made, is well, and yet
he who made it is not there. But in the things
which are held together by nature there is within
and there abides in them the power which made
them; wherefore the more it is fit to reverence
this power, and to think, that, if thou dost live
and act according to its will, everything in thee
is in conformity to intelligence. And thus also in
the universe, the things which belong to it are in
conformity to intelligence.

41. Whatever of the things which are not within thy power thou shalt suppose to be good for thee or evil, it must of necessity be that, if such a bad thing befall thee or the loss of such a good thing, thou wilt blame the gods, and hate men too, those who are the cause of the misfortune or the loss, or those who are suspected of being likely to be the cause ; and indeed we do much injustice, because we make a difference between these things [because we do not regard these things as indifferent]. But if we judge only those things which are in our power to be good or bad, there remains no reason either for finding fault with god or standing in a hostile attitude to man.

42. We are all working together to one end, some with knowledge and design, and others without knowing what they do ; as men also when they are asleep, of whom it is Heraclitus, I think, who says that they are laborers and co-operators in the things which take place in the universe. But men co-operate after different fashions : and even those co-operate abundantly, who find fault with what happens and those who try to oppose it and to hinder it ; for the universe had need even of such men as these. It remains then for thee to understand among what kind of

workmen thou placest thyself; for he who rules all things will certainly make a right use of thee, and he will receive thee among some part of the co-operators and of those whose labors conduce to one end. But be not thou such a part as the mean and ridiculous verse in the play, which Chrysippus speaks of.

43. Does the sun undertake to do the work of the rain, or Aesculapius the work of the Fruit-bearer [the earth]? And how is it with respect to each of the stars, are they not different and yet they work together to the same end?

44. If the gods have determined about me and about the things which must happen to me, they have determined well, for it is not easy even to imagine a deity without forethought; and as to doing me harm, why should they have any desire towards that? for what advantage would result to them from this or to the whole, which is the special object of their providence? But if they have not determined about me individually, they have certainly determined about the whole at least, and the things which happen by way of sequence in this general arrangement I ought to accept with pleasure and to be content with them. But if they determine about nothing — which it is wicked to believe, or if we do believe it, let us neither

12

sacrifice nor pray nor swear by them nor do any.
thing else which we do as if the gods were present
and lived with us — but if however the gods determine about none of the things which concern
us, I am able to determine about myself, and I
can inquire about that which is useful ; and that
is useful to every man which is conformable to
his own constitution and nature.   But my nature
is rational and social ; and my city and country,
so far as I am Antoninus, is Rome, but so far
as I am a man, it is the world.   The things then
which are useful to these cities are alone useful
to me.

45. Whatever happens to every man, this is for
the interest of the universal : this might be sufficient.   But further thou wilt observe this also as
a general truth, if thou dost observe, that whatever
is profitable to any man is profitable also to other
men.   But let the word profitable be taken here
in the common sense as said of things of the middle kind [neither good nor bad].

46. As it happens to thee in the amphitheatre
and such places, that the continual sight of the
same things and the uniformity make the spectacle
wearisome, so it is in the whole of life ; for all
things above, below, are the same and from **the**
same.   How long then ?

47. Think continually that all kinds of men and of all kinds of pursuits and of all nations are dead, so that thy thoughts come down even to Philistion and Phoebus and Origanion. Now turn thy thoughts to the other kinds [of men]. To that place then we must remove, where there are so many great orators, and so many noble philosophers, Heraclitus, Pythagoras, Socrates ; so many heroes of former days, and so many generals after them, and tyrants ; besides these, Eudoxus, Hipparchus, Archimedes, and other men of acute natural talents, great minds, lovers of labor, versatile, confident, mockers even of the perishable and ephemeral life of man, as Menippus and such as are like him. As to all these consider that they have long been in the dust. What harm then is this to them ; and what to those whose names are altogether unknown ? One thing here is worth a great deal, to pass thy life in truth and justice, with a benevolent disposition even to liars and unjust men.

48. When thou wishest to delight thyself, think of the virtues of those who live with thee ; for instance, the activity of one, and the modesty of another, and the liberality of a third, and some other good quality of a fourth. For nothing delights so much as the examples of the virtues,

when they are exhibited in the morals of those who live with us and present themselves in abundance, as far as is possible. Wherefore we must keep them before us.

49. Art thou dissatisfied because thou weighest only so many litrae and not three hundred? Be not dissatisfied then that thou must live only so many years and not more; for as thou art satisfied with the amount of substance which has been assigned to thee, so be content with the time.

50. Let us try to persuade them [men]. But act even against their will, when the principles of justice lead that way. If however any man by using force stands in thy way, betake thyself to contentment and tranquillity, and at the same time employ the hindrance towards the exercise of some other virtue; and remember that thy attempt was with a reservation [conditionally] that thou didst not desire to do impossibilities What then didst thou desire? — Some such effort as this — But thou attainest thy object, if the things to which thou wast moved are [not] accomplished.†

51. He who loves fame considers another man's activity to be his own good; and he who loves pleasure, his own sensations; but he who has

understanding, considers his own acts to be his own good.

52. It is in our power to have no opinion about a thing, and not to be disturbed in our soul; for things themselves have no natural power to form our judgments.

53. Accustom thyself to attend carefully to what is said by another, and as much as it is possible, be in the speaker's mind.

54. That which is not good for the swarm, neither is it good for the bee.

55. If sailors abused the helmsman or the sick the doctor, would they listen to anybody else; or how could the helmsman secure the safety of those in the ship or the doctor the health of those whom he attends?

56. How many together with whom I came into the world are already gone out of it.

57. To the jaundiced honey tastes bitter, and to those bitten by mad dogs water causes fear; and to little children the ball is a fine thing. Why then am I angry? Dost thou think that a false opinion has less power than the bile in the jaundiced or the poison in him who is bitten by a mad dog?

58. No man will hinder thee from living according to the reason of thy own nature: nothing

will happen to thee contrary to the reason of the universal nature.

59. What kind of people are those whom men wish to please, and for what objects, and by what kind of acts? How soon will time cover all things, and how many it has covered already.

VII.

WHAT is badness? It is that which thou hast often seen. And on the occasion of everything which happens keep this in mind, that it is that which thou hast often seen. Everywhere up and down thou wilt find the same things, with which the old histories are filled, those of the middle ages and those of our own day; with which cities and houses are filled now. There is nothing new: all things are both familiar and short-lived.

2. How can our principles become dead, unless the impressions [thoughts] which correspond to them are extinguished? But it is in thy power continuously to fan these thoughts into a flame. I can have that opinion about anything, which I ought to have. If I can, why am I disturbed? The things which are external to my mind have no relation at all to my mind. — Let this be the

state of thy affects, and thou standest erect. **To** recover thy life is in thy power. Look at things again as thou didst use to look at them ; for in this consists the recovery of thy life.

3. The idle business of show, plays on the stage, flocks of sheep, herds, exercises with spears, a bone cast to little dogs, a bit of bread into fish-ponds, laborings of ants and burden-carrying, runnings about of frightened little mice, puppets pulled by strings — [all alike]. It is thy duty then in the midst of such things to show good humor and not a proud air ; to understand however that every man is worth just so much as the things are worth about which he busies himself.

4. In discourse thou must attend to what is said, and in every movement thou must observe what is doing. And in the one thou shouldst see immediately to what end it refers, but in the other watch carefully what is the thing signified.

5. Is my understanding sufficient for this or not ? If it is sufficient, I use it for the work as an instrument given by the universal nature. But if it is not sufficient, then either I retire from the work and give way to him who is able to do it better, unless there be some reason why I ought not to do so ; or I do it as well as I can, taking to help me the man who with the aid of my ruling

principle can do what is now fit and useful for the
general good. For whatsoever either by myself
or with another I can do, ought to be directed to
this only, to that which is useful and well suited
to society.

6. How many after being celebrated by fame
have been given up to oblivion; and how many
who have celebrated the fame of others have long
been dead.

7. Be not ashamed to be helped; for it is thy
business to do thy duty like a soldier in the assault
on a town. How then, if being lame thou canst
not mount up on the battlements alone, but with
the help of another it is possible?

8. Let not future things disturb thee, for thou
wilt come to them, if it shall be necessary, having
with thee the same reason which now thou usest
for present things.

9. All things are implicated with one another,
and the bond is holy; and there is hardly anything
unconnected with any other thing. For things
have been co-ordinated, and they combine to form
the same universe [order]. For there is one
universe made up of all things, and one god who
pervades all things, and one substance, and one
law, [one] common reason in all intelligent animals, and one truth; if indeed there is also one

perfection for all animals which are of the same stock and participate in the same reason.

10. Everything material soon disappears in the substance of the whole; and everything formal [causal] is very soon taken back into the universal reason; and the memory of everything is very soon overwhelmed in time.

11. To the rational animal the same act is according to nature and according to reason.

12. Be thou erect, or be made erect. (III. 5.)

13. Just as it is with the members in those bodies which are united in one, so it is with rational beings which exist separate, for they have been constituted for one co-operation. And the perception of this will be more apparent to thee, if thou often sayest to thyself that I am a member [μέλος] of the system of rational beings. But if [using the letter r] thou sayest that thou art a part [μέρος], thou dost not yet love men from thy heart; beneficence does not yet delight thee for its own sake;[1] thou still doest it barely as a thing of propriety, and not yet as doing good to thyself.

14. Let there fall externally what will on the parts which can feel the effects of this fall. For

---

[1] I have used Gataker's conjecture καταληκτικῶς instead of the common reading καταληπτικῶς: compare IV. 20; IX. 42.

those parts which have felt will complain, if they choose. But I, unless I think that what has happened is an evil, am not injured. And it is in my power not to think so.

15. Whatever any one does or says, I must be good, just as if the gold, or the emerald or the purple were always saying this, Whatever any one does or says, I must be emerald and keep my color.

16. The ruling faculty does not disturb itself, I mean, does not frighten itself or cause itself pain.† But if any one else can frighten or pain it, let him do so. For the faculty itself will not by its own opinion turn itself into such ways. Let the body itself take care, if it can, that it suffer nothing, and let it speak, if it suffers. But the soul itself, that which is subject to fear, to pain, which has completely the power of forming an opinion about these things, will suffer nothing, for it will never deviate † into such a judgment. The leading principle in itself wants nothing, unless it makes a want for itself; and therefore it is both free from perturbation and unimpeded, if it does not disturb and impede itself.

17. Eudaemonia [happiness] is a good daemon, or a good thing. What then art thou doing here, O imagination? go away, I intreat thee by the

gods, as thou didst come, for I want thee not.
But thou art come according to thy old fashion
I am not angry with thee : only go away.

18. Is any man afraid of change ?   Why what
can take place without change ?   What then is
more pleasing or more suitable to the universal
nature ?   And canst thou take a bath unless the
wood undergoes a change? and canst thou be
nourished, unless the food undergoes a change?
And can anything else that is useful be accomplished without change ?   Dost thou not see then
that for thyself also to change is just the same,
and equally necessary for the universal nature ?

19. Through the universal substance as through
a furious torrent all bodies are carried, being by
their nature united with and co-operating with the
whole, as the parts of our body with one another.
How many a Chrysippus, how many a Socrates,
how many an Epictetus has time already swallowed up ?   And let the same thought occur to
thee with reference to every man and thing.

20. One thing only troubles me, lest I should
do something which the constitution of man does
not allow, or in the way which it does not allow,
or what it does not allow now.

21. Near is thy forgetfulness of all things ;
and near the forgetfulness of thee by all.

22. It is peculiar to man to love even those who do wrong. And this happens, if when they do wrong it occurs to thee that they are kinsmen, and that they do wrong through ignorance and unintentionally, and that soon both of you will die ; and above all, that the wrong doer has done thee no harm, for he has not made thy ruling faculty worse than it was before.

23. The universal nature out of the universal substance, as if it were wax, now moulds a horse, and when it has broken this up, it uses the material for a tree, then for a man, then for something else ; and each of these things subsists for a very short time. But it is no hardship for the vessel to be broken up, just as there was none in its being fastened together.

24. A scowling look is altogether unnatural ; when it is often assumed,[2] the result is that all comeliness dies away, and at last is so completely extinguished that it cannot be again lighted up at all. Try to conclude from this very fact that it is contrary to reason. For if even the perception of doing wrong shall depart, what reason is there for living any longer ?

25. Nature which governs the whole will soon change all things which thou seest, and out of their

[2] This is corrupt.

substance will make other things, and again other things from the substance of them, in order that the world may be ever new.

26. When a man has done thee any wrong, immediately consider with what opinion) about good or evil he has done wrong. For when thou hast seen this, thou wilt pity him, and wilt neither wonder nor be angry. For either thou thyself thinkest the same thing to be good that he does or another thing of the same kind. It is thy duty then to pardon him. But if thou dost not think such things to be good or evil, thou wilt more readily be well disposed to him who is in error.

27. Think not so much of what thou hast not as of what thou hast: but of the things which thou hast select the best, and then reflect how eagerly they would have been sought, if thou hadst them not. At the same time however take care that thou dost not through being so pleased with them accustom thyself to overvalue them, so as to be disturbed if ever thou shouldst not have them.

28. Retire into thyself. The rational principle which rules has this nature, that it is content with itself when it does what is just, and so secures tranquillity.

29. Wipe out the imagination. Stop the pull-

ing of the strings. Confine thyself to the present. Understand well what happens either to thee or to another. Divide and distribute every object into the causal [formal] and the material. Think of thy last hour. Let the wrong which is done by a man stay there where the wrong was done.

30. Direct thy attention to what is said. Let thy understanding enter into the things that are doing and the things which do them. (VII. 4.)

31. Adorn thyself with simplicity and modesty and with indifference towards the things which lie between virtue and vice. Love mankind. Follow god. The poet says that Law rules all — † And it is enough to remember that law rules all.† [8] —

32. About death: whether it is a dispersion, or a resolution into atoms, or annihilation, it is either extinction or change.

33. About pain: the pain which is intolerable carries us off; but that which lasts a long time is tolerable; and the mind maintains its own tranquillity by retiring into itself,† and the ruling faculty is not made worse. But the parts which are harmed by pain, let them, if they can, give their opinion about it.

---

[8] The end of this section is unintelligible.

34. About fame : look at the minds [of those who seek fame], observe what they are, and what kind of things they avoid, and what kind of things they pursue. And consider that as the heaps of sand piled on one another hide the former sands, so in life the events which go before are soon covered by those which come after.

35. From Plato :[4] the man who has an elevated mind and takes a view of all time and of all substance, dost thou suppose it possible for him to think that human life is anything great? it is not possible, he said. — Such a man then will think that death also is no evil — Certainly not.

36. From Antisthenes : It is royal to do good and to be abused.

37. It is a base thing for the countenance to be obedient and to regulate and compose itself as the mind commands, and for the mind not to be regulated and composed by itself.

38. It is not right to vex ourselves at things,
For they care nought about it.[5]

39. To the immortal gods and us give joy.

40. Life must be reaped like the ripe ears of corn :
One man is born ; another dies.[6]

[4] Plato, Pol. vi. 486.
[5] From the Bellerophon of Euripides.
[6] From the Hypsipyle of Euripides. Cicero (Tuscul.

41. If gods care not for me and for my children,
There is a reason for it.

42. For the good is with me, and the just.[7]

43. No joining others in their wailing, no
violent emotion.

44. From Plato:[8] But I would make this man
a sufficient answer, which is this : Thou sayest
not well, if thou thinkest that a man, who is good
for anything at all ought to compute the hazard
of life or death, and should not rather look to this
only in all that he does, whether he is doing what
is just or unjust, and the works of a good or a
bad man.

45. [8] For thus it is, men of Athens, in truth.
wherever a man has placed himself thinking it the
best place for him, or has been placed by a commander, there in my opinion he ought to stay and
to abide the hazard, taking nothing into the
reckoning, either death or anything else, before
the baseness [of deserting his post].

46. But, my good friend, consider whether that

III. 25.) has translated six lines from Euripides, and
among them are these two lines : —

> Reddenda terrae est terra : tum vita omnibus
> Metenda ut fruges : Sic jubet necessitas.

[7] See Aristophanes, Acharnenses.
[8] From the Apologia.

13

which is noble and good is not something different
from saving and being saved; for †we must not
allow that it consists in living such or such a time,
at least for one who is really a man; † and he
should not be fond of life, but entrusting this to
god and believing what the women say, that no
man can escape his destiny, he should next inquire how he may best live the time that he has
to live.[9]

47. Look round at the courses of the stars, as
if thou wert going along with them; and constantly consider the changes of the elements into
one another; for such thoughts purge away the
filth of the terrene life.

48. This is a fine saying of Plato:[10] That he
who is discoursing about men should look also at
earthly things as if he viewed them from some
higher place; should look at them in their as-
semblies, armies, agricultural labors, marriages,
treaties, births, deaths, noise of the courts of
justice, desert places, various nations of barba-

[9] Plato, Gorgias, c. 68. In this passage the text of
Antoninus has ἐατέον, which is perhaps right; but there
seems to be something wrong in the text. It is certainly
difficult to see the exact construction of parts of the
section. The reading εὐκτέον for εἀτέον does not mend
the matter.

[10] It is not in the extant writings of Plato.

rians, feasts, lamentations, markets, a mixture of
all things and an orderly combination of contraries.

49. Consider the past; such great changes of
political supremacies. Thou mayest foresee also
the things which will be. For they will certainly
be of like form, and it is not possible that they
should deviate from the order of the things which
take place now: accordingly to have contemplated
human life for forty years is the same as to have
contemplated it for ten thousand years. For
what more wilt thou see?

50. That which has grown from the earth to
the earth,
But that which has sprung from heavenly seed,
Back to the heavenly realms returns.[11]

This is either a dissolution of the mutual involution of the atoms, or a similar dispersion of the
unsentient elements.

51. With food and drinks and cunning magic
arts
Turning the channel's course to 'scape from
death.[12]
The breeze which heaven has sent
We must endure, and toil without complaining.

[11] From the Chrysippus of Euripides.
[12] The first two lines are from the Supp. of Euripides, v. 1110.

52. Another may be more expert in casting his opponent; but let him not be more social, nor more modest, nor better disciplined to meet all that happens, nor more considerate with respect to the faults of his neighbors.

53. Where any work can be done conformably to the reason which is common to gods and men, there we have nothing to fear: for where we are able to get profit by means of the activity which is successful and proceeds according to our constitution, there no harm is to be suspected.

54. Everywhere and at all times it is in thy power piously to acquiesce in thy present condition, and to behave justly to those who are about thee, and to exert thy skill upon thy present thoughts, that nothing shall steal into them without being well examined.

55. Do not look around thee to discover other men's ruling principles, but look straight to this, to what nature leads thee, both the universal nature through the things which happen to thee, and thy own nature through the acts which must be done by thee. But every being ought to do that which is according to its constitution; and all other things have been made for the sake of rational beings, just as among irrational things the inferior for the sake of the superior, but the rational for the sake of one another.

The prime principle then in man's constitution
is the social. And the second is not to yield to
the persuasions of the body, for it is the peculiar
office of the rational and intelligent motion to circumscribe itself, and never to be overpowered
either by the motion of the senses or of the appetites, for both are animal; but the intelligent
motion claims superiority and does not permit
itself to be overpowered by the others. And with
good reason, for it is formed by nature to use all
of them. The third thing in the rational constitution is freedom from error and from deception.
Let then the ruling principle holding fast to these
things go straight on, and it has what is its own.

56. Consider thyself to be dead, and to have
completed thy life up to the present time; and
live according to nature the remainder which is
allowed thee.

57. Love that only which happens to thee, and
is spun with the thread of thy destiny. For what
is more suitable?

58. In everything which happens keep before
thy eyes those to whom the same things happened, and how they were vexed, and treated
them as strange things, and found fault with
them: and now where are they? Nowhere.
Why then dost thou choose to act in the same

way? and why dost thou not leave these agita-
tions which are foreign to nature, to those who
cause them and those who are moved by them?
and why art thou not altogether intent upon the
right way of making use of the things which happen to thee? for then thou wilt use them well,
and they will be a material for thee [to work on].
Only attend to thyself, and resolve to be a good
man in every act which thou doest: and remember   *   *   *   *   *.[13]

59. Look within. Within is the fountain of
good, and it will ever bubble up, if thou wilt ever
dig.

60. The body ought to be compact, and to show
no irregularity either in motion or attitude. For
what the mind shows in the face by maintaining
in it the expression of intelligence and propriety,
that ought to be required also in the whole body.
But all these things should be observed without
affectation.

61. The art of life is more like the wrestler's
art than the dancer's, in respect of this that it
should stand ready and firm to meet onsets which
are sudden and unexpected.

[13] This section is obscure, and the conclusion is so
corrupt that it is impossible to give any probable meaning to it. It is better to leave it as it is than to patch it
up, as some critics and translators have done.

62. Constantly observe who those are whose approbation thou wishest to have, and what ruling principles they possess. For then thou wilt neither blame those who offend involuntarily, nor wilt thou want their approbation, if thou lookest to the sources of their opinions and appetites.

63. Every soul, the philosopher says, is involuntarily deprived of truth; consequently in the same way it is deprived of justice and temperance and benevolence and everything of the kind. It is most necessary to bear this constantly in mind, for thus thou wilt be more gentle towards all.

64. In every pain let this thought be present, that there is no dishonor in it, nor does it make the governing intelligence worse, for it does not damage the intelligence either so far as the intelligence is rational [14] or so far as it is social. Indeed in the case of most pains let this remark of Epicurus aid thee, that pain is neither intolerable nor everlasting, if thou bearest in mind that it has its limits, and if thou addest nothing to it in imagination: and remember this too, that we do not

---

[14] The text has ὑλική, which it has been proposed to alter to λογική, and this change is necessary. We shall then have in this section λογική and κοινωνική associated, as we have in s. 63 λογική and πολιτική, and in s. 72.

perceive that many things which are disagreeable
to us are the same as pain, such as excessive
drowsiness, and the being scorched by heat, and
the having no appetite. When then thou art discontented about any of these things, say to thyself, that thou art yielding to pain.

65. Take care not to feel towards the inhuman,
as they feel towards men.[15]

66. How do we know if Telauges was not superior in character to Socrates? for it is not enough
that Socrates died a more noble death, and dis-
puted more skilfully with the sophists, and passed
the night in the cold with more endurance, and
that when he was bid to arrest Leon of Salamis,
he considered it more noble to refuse, and that he
walked in a swaggering way in the streets —
though as to this one may have great doubts if it
was true. But we ought to inquire, what kind
of a soul it was that Socrates possessed, and if he
was able to be content with being just towards
men and pious towards the gods, neither idly
vexed on account of men's villany, nor yet making himself a slave to any man's ignorance, nor
receiving as strange anything that fell to his

---

[15] I have followed Gataker's conjecture οἱ ἀπάνθρωτο·
instead of the MSS. reading οἱ ἄνθρωποι.

share out of the universal nor enduring it as intolerable, nor allowing his understanding to sympathize with the affects of the miserable flesh

67. Nature has not so mingled † [the intelligence] with the composition of the body, as not to have allowed thee the power of circumscribing thyself and of bringing under subjection to thyself all that is thy own ; for it is very possible to be a divine man and to be recognized as such by no one. Always bear this in mind ; and another thing too, that very little indeed is necessary for living a happy life. And because thou hast despaired of becoming a dialectician and skilled in the knowledge of nature, do not for this reason renounce the hope of being both free and modest and social and obedient to god.

68. It is in thy power to live free from all compulsion in the greatest tranquillity of mind, even if all the world cry out against thee as much as hey choose, and even if wild beasts tear in pieces the members of this kneaded matter which has grown around thee. For what hinders the mind in the midst of all this from maintaining itself in tranquillity and in a just judgment of all surrounding things and in a ready use of the objects which are presented to it, so that the judgment may say to the thing which falls under its obser-

vation ; This thou art in substance [reality], though in men's opinion thou mayst appear to be of a different kind ; and the use shall say to that which falls under the hand : Thou art the thing that I was seeking ; for to me that which presents itself is always a material for virtue both rational and political, and in a word for the exercise of art which belongs to man or god. For everything which happens has a relationship either to god or man, and is neither new nor difficult to handle, but usual and apt matter to work on.

69. The perfection of moral character consists in this, in passing every day as the last, and in being neither violently excited nor torpid nor playing the hypocrite.

70. The gods who are immortal are not vexed because during so long a time they must tolerate continually men such as they are and so many of them bad ; and besides this they also take care of them in all ways. But thou, who art destined to end so soon, art thou wearied of enduring the bad, and this too when thou art one of them ?

71. It is a ridiculous thing for a man not to fly from his own badness, which is indeed possible, but to fly from other men's badness, which is impossible.

72. Whatever the rational and political [social] faculty finds to be neither intelligent nor social, it properly judges to be inferior to itself.

73. When thou hast done a good act and another has received it, why dost thou still look for a third thing besides these, as fools do, either to have the reputation of having done a good act or to obtain a return?

74. No man is tired of receiving what is useful. But it is useful to act according to nature. Do not then be tired of receiving what is useful by doing it to others.

75. The nature of the All moved to make the universe. But now either everything that takes place comes by way of consequence [or continuity]; or even the chief things towards which the ruling power of the universe directs its own movement are governed by no rational principle. If this is remembered it will make thee more tranquil in many things. (IX. 21, VI. 44.) [16]

---

[16] It is not easy to understand this section. It has been suggested that there is some error in ἢ ἀλόγιστα, &c. Some of the translators have made nothing of the passage, and they have somewhat perverted the words. The first proposition is, that the universe was made by some sufficient power. A beginning of the universe is assumed, and a power which framed an order. The

next question is, How are things produced now ; or in
other words, by what power do forms appear in continuous succession ?   The answer, according to Antoninus,
may be this : It is by virtue of the original constitution
of things that all change and succession have been
effected and are effected.   And this is intelligible in a
sense, if we admit that the universe is always one and
the same, a continuity of identity ; as much one and
the same as man is one and the same, which he believes
himself to be, though he also believes and cannot help
believing that both in his body and in his thoughts there
is change and succession.   There is no real discontinu-
ity then in the universe ; and if we say that there was
an order framed in the beginning and that the things
which are now produced are a consequence of a pre-
vious arrangement, we speak of things as we are compelled to view them, as forming a series or succession ;
just as we speak of the changes in our own bodies and
the sequence of our own thoughts.   But as there are
no intervals, not even intervals infinitely small, between
any two supposed states of any one thing, so there are
no intervals, not even infinitely small, between what we
call one thing and any other thing which we speak of
as immediately preceding or following it.   What we call
time is an idea derived from our notion of a succession
of things or events, an idea which is a part of our constitution, but not an idea which we can suppose to belong to an infinite intelligence and power.   The conclusion then is certain that the present and the past, the
production of present things and the supposed original
order, out of which we say that present things now
come, are one : and the present productive power and

ANTONINUS. VII.

for one thing. I suppose then that Antoninus wrote
here as people sometimes talk now, and that his real
meaning is not exactly expressed by his words. There
are certainly other passages from which, I think, that
we may collect that he had notions of production something like what I have expressed.

We now come to the alternative: "or even the chief
things . . . . . . principle." I do not exactly know what
he means by τὰ κυριώτατα, "the chief," or, "the most
excellent," or whatever it is. But as he speaks elsewhere of inferior and superior things, and of the inferior being for the use of the superior, and of rational
beings being the highest, he may here mean rational
beings. He also in this alternative assumes a governing
power of the universe, and that it acts by directing its
power towards these chief objects, or making its special,
proper, motion towards them. And here he uses the
noun (ὁρμή) "movement," which contains the same
notion as the verb (ὥρμησε) "moved," which he used at
the beginning of the paragraph when he was speaking
of the making of the universe. If we do not accept the
first hypothesis, he says, we must take the conclusion
of the second, that the "chief things towards which the
ruling power of the universe makes a movement are
directed by no rational principle." The meaning then
is, if there is a meaning in it, that though there is a
governing power, which strives to give effect to its
efforts, we must conclude that there is no rational direction of anything, if the power which first made the universe does not in some way govern it still. Besides, if
we assume that anything is now produced or now exists

without the action of the supreme intelligence, and yet
that this intelligence makes an effort to act, we obtain a
conclusion which cannot be reconciled with the nature
of a supreme power, whose existence Antoninus always
assumes. The tranquillity that a man may gain from
these reflections must result from his rejecting the second hypothesis, and accepting the first ; whatever may
be the exact sense in which the emperor understood the
first. Or, as he says elsewhere, if there is no providence which governs the world, man has at least the
power of governing himself according to the constitution of his nature ; and so he may be tranquil, if he
does the best that he can.

If there is no error in the passage, it is worth the
labor to discover the writer's exact meaning ; for I think
that he had a meaning, though people may not agree
what it was. (Compare IX. 28.) If I have rightly explained the emperor's meaning in this and other pas
sages, he has touched the solution of a great question.

VIII.

THIS reflection also tends to the removal of the desire of empty fame, that it is no longer in thy power to have lived the whole of thy life, or at least thy life from thy youth upwards, like a philosopher : but both to many others and to thyself it is plain that thou art far from philosophy. Thou hast fallen into disorder then, so that it is no longer easy for thee to get the reputation of a philosopher ; and thy plan of life also opposes it. If then thou hast truly seen where the matter lies, throw away the thought, How thou shalt seem [to others], and be content if thou shalt live the rest of thy life in such wise as thy nature wills. Observe then what it wills, and let nothing else distract thee ; for thou hast had experience of many wanderings without having found happiness anywhere, not in syllogisms, nor in wealth, nor in reputation, nor in enjoyment, nor anywhere. Where is it then ? In doing what man's nature requires. How then shall a man do this? **If he** has principles from which come his affects and his acts. What principles? Those which relate to good and bad : the belief that there is nothing good for man, which does not make him just, temperate, manly, free ; and that there is nothing bad, which does not do the contrary to what has been mentioned.

2. On the occasion of every act ask thyself, How is this with respect to me? Shall I repent of it? A little time and I am dead, and all is gone. What more do I seek, if what I am now doing is the work of an intelligent living being, and a social being, and one who is under the same law with god?

3. Alexander and Caius and Pompeius, what are they in comparison with Diogenes and Heraclitus and Socrates? For they were acquainted with things, and their causes [forms], and their matter, and the ruling principles of these men were the same [or conformable to their pursuits]. But as to the others, how many things had they to care for, and to how many things were they slaves.

4. [Consider] that men will do the same things nevertheless, even though thou shouldst burst.

5. This is the chief thing : Be not perturbed,

for all things are according to the nature of the universal ; and in a little time thou wilt be nobody and nowhere, like Hadrianus and Augustus. In the next place having fixed thy eyes steadily on thy business look at it, and at the same time remembering that it is thy duty to be a good man, and what man's nature demands, do it without turning aside ; and speak as it seems to thee most just, only let it be with good temper and with modesty and without hypocrisy.

6. The nature of the universal has this work to do, to remove to that place the things which are in this, to change them, to take them away here and to carry them there. All things are change, yet we need not fear anything new. All things are familiar [to us] ; but the distribution of them also remains the same.

7. Every nature is contented with itself when it goes on its way well ; and a rational nature goes on its way well, when in its thoughts it assents to nothing false or uncertain, and when it directs its movements to social acts only, and when it confines its desires and aversions to the things which are in its power, and when it is satisfied with everything that is assigned to it by the common nature. For of this common nature every particular nature is a part, as the nature

14

of the leaf is a part of the nature of the plant ;
except that in the plant the nature of the leaf is
part of a nature 'which has not perception or
reason, and is subject to be impeded ; but the
nature of man is part of a nature which is not
subject to impediments, and is intelligent and
just, since it gives to everything in equal portions
and according to its worth times, substance, cause
·[form]. activity, and incident. But examine, not
to discover that any one thing compared with any
other single thing is equal in all respects, but by
taking all the parts together of one thing and
comparing them with all the parts together of
another.

8. Thou hast not leisure [or ability] to read
But thou hast leisure [or ability] to check arrogance : thou hast leisure to be superior to pleasure
and pain : thou hast leisure to be superior to love
of fame, and not to be vexed at stupid and ungrateful people, nay even to care for them.

9. Let no man any longer hear thee finding
fault with the court life or with thy own. (v. 16.)

10. Repentance is a kind of self-reproof for
having neglected something useful ; but that
which is good must be something useful, and the
perfect good man should look after it. But no
such man would ever repent of having refused

any sensual pleasure. Pleasure then is neither good nor useful.

11. This thing, what is it in itself, in its own constitution? What is its substance and material? And what its causal nature [or form]? And what is it doing in the world? And how long does it subsist?

12. When thou risest from sleep with reluctance, remember that it is according to thy constitution and according to human nature to perform social acts, but sleeping is common also to irrational animals. But that which is according to each individual's nature, is also more peculiarly its own, and more suitable to its nature, and indeed also more agreeable.

13. Constantly, and, if it be possible, on the occasion of every impression on the soul, apply to it the principles of Physic, of Moral and of Dialectic.

14. Whatever man thou meetest with, immediately say to thyself: What opinions has this man about good and bad? For if with respect to pleasure and pain and the causes of each, and with respect to fame and ignominy, death and life he has such and such opinions, it will seem nothing wonderful or strange to me. if he does such and such things; and I shall bear in mind that he is compelled to do so.

15. Remember that as it is a shame to be surprised if the fig-tree produces figs, so it is to be
surprised if the world produces such and such
things of which it is productive ; and for the
physician and the helmsman it is a shame to be
surprised, if a man has a fever, or if the wind is
unfavorable.

16. Remember that to change thy opinion and
to follow him who corrects thy error is as consistent with freedom as it is to persist in thy error.
For it is thy own, the activity which is exerted
according to thy own movement and judgment,
and indeed according to thy own understanding
too.

17. If a thing is in thy own power, why dost
thou do it? but if it is in the power of another,
whom dost thou blame? the atoms [chance] or
the gods? Both are foolish. Thou must blame
nobody. For if thou canst, correct [that which is
the cause] ; but if thou canst not do this, correct
at least the thing itself; but if thou canst not do
even this, of what use is it to thee to find fault?
for nothing should be done without a purpose.

18. That which has died falls not out of the
universe. If it stays here, it also changes here,
and is dissolved into its proper parts, which are
elements of the universe and of thyself. And
these too change, and they murmur not.

19. Everything exists for some end, a horse, a vine. Why dost thou wonder? Even the sun will say, I am for some purpose, and the rest of the gods will say the same. For what purpose then art thou? to enjoy pleasure? See if common sense allows this.

20. Nature has had regard in everything no less to the end than to the beginning and the continuance, just like the man who throws up a ball. What good is it then for the ball to be thrown up, or harm for it to come down, or even to have fallen? and what good is it to the bubble while it holds together, or what harm when it is burst? The same may be said of a light also.

21. Turn it [the body] inside out, and see what kind of thing it is; and when it has grown old, what kind of thing it becomes, and when it is diseased.

Short lived are both the praiser and the praised, and the rememberer and the remembered: and all this in a nook of this part of the world; and not even here do all agree, no not any one with himself: and the whole earth too is a point.

22. Attend to the matter which is before thee, whether it is an opinion or an act or a word.

Thou sufferest this justly: for thou choosest

rather to become good to-morrow than to be good
to-day.

23. Am I doing anything? I do it with reference to the good of mankind. Does anything
happen to me? I receive it and refer it to the
gods, and the source of all things, from which all
that happens is derived.

24. Such as bathing appears to thee — oil,
sweat, dirt, filthy water, all things disgusting, —
so is every part of life and everything.

25. Lucilla saw Verus die, and then Lucilla
died. Secunda saw Maximus die, and then Secunda died. Epitynchanus saw Diotimus die,
and then Epitynchanus died. Antoninus saw
Faustina die, and then Antoninus died. Such is
everything. Celer saw Hadrianus die, and then
Celer died. And those sharp-witted men, either
seers or men inflated with pride, where are they?
for instance the sharp-witted men, Charax and
Demetrius the Platonist and Eudaemon, and any
one else like them. All ephemeral, dead long
ago. Some indeed have not been remembered
even for a short time, and others have become the
heroes of fables, and again others have disappeared
even from fables. Remember this then, that this
little compound, thyself, must either be dissolved,
or thy poor breath must be extinguished, or be
removed and placed elsewhere.

26. It is satisfaction to a man to do the proper works of a man. Now it is a proper work of a man to be benevolent to his own kind, to despise the movements of the senses, to form a just judgment of plausible appearances, and to take a survey of the nature of the universe and of the things which happen in it.

27. There are three relations [between thee and other things]: the one to the body[1] which surrounds thee; the second to the divine cause from which all things come to all; and the third to those who live with thee.

28. Pain is either an evil to the body — then let the body say what it thinks of it — or to the soul; but it is in the power of the soul to maintain its own serenity and tranquillity, and not to think that pain is an evil. For every judgment and movement and desire and aversion is within, and no evil ascends so high.

29. Wipe out thy imaginations by often saying to thyself: now it is in my power to let no badness be in this soul, nor desire nor any perturbation at all; but looking at all things I see what is

[1] The text has αἴτιον which in Antoninus means "form," "formal." Accordingly Schulze recommends either Valkenaer's emendation ἀγγεῖον, "body," or Corae's σωμάτιον. Compare XII. 13, X. 38.

their nature, and I use each according to its value. — Remember this power which thou hast from nature.

30. Speak both in the senate and to every man, whoever he may be, appropriately, not with any affectation : use plain discourse.

31. Augustus' court, wife, daughter, descendants, ancestors, sister, Agrippa, kinsmen, intimates, friends, Arius, Maecenas, physicians and sacrificing priests — the whole court is dead. Then turn to the rest, not considering the death of a single man, [but of a whole race,] as of the Pompeii ; and that which is inscribed on the tombs, The last of his race. Consider what trouble those before them have had that they might leave a successor ; and then, that of necessity some one must be the last. Again here consider the death of a whole race.

32. It is thy duty to order thy life well in every single act ; and if every act does its duty, as far as is possible, be content ; and no one is able to hinder thee so that each act shall not do its duty — But something external will stand in the way — Nothing will stand in the way of thy acting justly and soberly and considerately — But perhaps some other active power will be hindered —Well, but by acquiescing in the hindrance and by being content

to transfer thy efforts to that which is allowed.
another opportunity of action is immediately put
before thee in place of that which was hindered.
and one which will adapt itself to this order of
which we are speaking.

33. Receive [wealth or prosperity] without
arrogance; and be ready to let it go.

34. If thou didst ever see a hand cut off, or a
foot, or a head, lying anywhere apart from the
rest of the body, such does a man make himself,
as far as he can, who is not content with what
happens, and separates himself from others, or
does anything unsocial. Suppose that thou hast
detached thyself from the natural unity — for
thou wast made by nature a part, but now thou
hast cut thyself off — yet here there is this
beautiful provision, that it is in thy power again to
unite thyself. God has allowed this to no other
part, after it has been separated and cut asunder.
to come together again. But consider the benevolence with which he has distinguished man, for
he has put it in his power not to be separated at
all from the universal; and when he has been
separated, he has allowed him to return and to be
united and to resume his place as a part.

35. As the nature of the universal has given
to every rational being all the other powers that

it has,† so we have received from it this power
also. For as the universal nature converts and
fixes in its predestined place everything which
stands in its way and opposes it, and makes such
things a part of itself, so also the rational animal
is able to make every hindrance its own material,
and to use it for such purpose as it may have
designed.[2]

36. Do not disturb thyself by thinking of the
whole of thy life. Let not thy thoughts at once
embrace all the various troubles which thou mayst
expect to befall thee: but on every occasion ask
thyself, What is there in this which is intolerable
and past bearing? for thou wilt be ashamed to
confess. In the next place remember that neither
the future nor the past pains thee, but only the
present. But this is reduced to a very little, if
thou only circumscribest it, and chidest thy mind,
if it is unable to hold out against even this.

37. Does Panthea or Pergamus now sit by the
tomb of Verus?[3] Does Chaurias or Diotimus sit

---

[2] The text is corrupt at the beginning of the paragraph, but the meaning will appear if the second λογικὸν
is changed into ὅλων: though this change alone will not
establish the grammatical completeness of the text.

[3] "Verus" is a conjecture of Saumaise, and perhaps
the true reading.

by the tomb of Hadrianus? That would be ridiculous. Well, suppose they did sit there, would
the dead be conscious of it? and if the dead were
conscious, would they be pleased? and -if they
were pleased, would that make them immortal?
Was it not in the order of destiny that these persons too should become old women and old men
and then die? What then would those do after
these were dead? All this is foul smell and
blood in a bag.

38. If thou canst see sharp, look and judge
wisely.† says the philosopher.

39. In the constitution of the rational animal I
see no virtue which is opposed to justice ; but I
see a virtue which is opposed to love of pleasure,
and that is temperance.

40. If thou takest away thy opinion about that
which appears to give thee pain, thou thyself
standest in perfect security — Who is this? self —
The reason — But I am not reason — Be it so.
Let then the reason itself not trouble itself. But
if any other part of thee suffers, let it have its
own opinion about itself. (vii. 16.)

41. Hindrance to the perceptions of sense is
an evil to the animal nature. Hindrance to the
movements [desires] is equally an evil to the
animal nature. And something else also is equally

an impediment and an evil to the constitution of plants. So then that which is a hindrance to the intelligence is an evil to the intelligent nature. Apply all these things then to thyself. Does pain or sensuous pleasure affect thee? The senses will look to that. — Has any obstacle opposed thee in thy efforts towards an object? if indeed thou wast making this effort absolutely [unconditionally, or, without any reservation], certainly this obstacle is an evil to thee considered as a rational animal. But if thou takest [into consideration] the usual course of things, thou hast not yet been injured nor even impeded. The things however which are proper to the understanding no one is used to impede, for neither fire nor iron nor tyrant nor abuse touches it in any way. When it has been made a sphere, it continues a sphere. (XI. 12.)

42. It is not fit that I should give myself pain, for I have never intentionally given pain even to another.

43. Different things delight different people. But it is my delight to keep the ruling faculty sound without turning away either from any man or from any of the things which happen to men, but looking at and receiving all with welcome eyes and using everything according to its value.

44. See that thou secure this present time to thyself: for those who rather pursue posthumous fame do not consider that the men of after time will be exactly such as these whom they cannot bear now; and both are mortal. And what is it in any way to thee if these men of after time utter this or that sound or have this or that opinion about thee?

45. Take me and cast me where thou wilt; for there I shall keep my divine part tranquil, that is, content, if it can feel and act conformably to its proper constitution. Is this [change of place] sufficient reason why my soul should be unhappy and worse than it was, depressed, expanded, shrinking, affrighted? and what wilt thou find which is sufficient reason for this? [4]

46. Nothing can happen to any man which is not a human accident, nor to an ox which is not according to the nature of an ox, nor to a vine which is not according to the nature of a vine, nor to a stone which is not proper to a stone. If then there happens to each thing both what is usual and natural, why shouldst thou complain? For

---

[4] ὀρεγομένη in this passage seems to have a passive sense. It is difficult to find an apt expression for it and some of the other words. A comparison with xi. 12. will help to explain the meaning.

the common nature brings nothing which may not be borne by thee.

47. If thou art pained by any external thing, it is not this thing that disturbs thee, but thy own judgment about it. And it is in thy power to wipe out this judgment now. But if anything in thy own disposition gives thee pain, who hinders thee from correcting thy opinion? And even if thou art pained because thou art not doing some particular thing which seems to thee to be right, why dost thou not rather act than complain?— But some insuperable obstacle is in the way?— Do not be grieved then, for the cause of its not being done depends not on thee — But it is not worth while to live, if this cannot be done — Take thy departure then from life contentedly, just as he dies who is in full activity, and well-pleased too with the things which are obstacles.

48. Remember that the ruling faculty is invincible, when self-collected it is satisfied with itself, if it does nothing which it does not choose to do, even if it resist from mere obstinacy. What then will it be when it forms a judgment about anything aided by reason and deliberately? therefore the mind which is free from passions is a citadel, for man has nothing more secure to which he can fly for refuge and for the future be inexpugnable.

He then who has not seen this is an ignorant man ; but he who has seen it and does not fly to this refuge is unhappy.

49. Say nothing more to thyself than what the first appearances report. Suppose that it has been reported to thee that a certain person speaks ill of thee. This has been reported ; but that thou hast been injured, that has not been reported. I see that my child is sick. I do see ; but that he is in danger, I do not see. Thus then always abide by the first appearances, and add nothing thyself from within, and then nothing happens to thee. Or rather add something, like a man who knows everything that happens in the world.

50. A cucumber is bitter — Throw it away. — There are briers in the road — Turn aside from them. — This is enough. Do not add, And why were such things made in the world ? For thou wilt be ridiculed by a man who is acquainted with nature, as thou wouldst be ridiculed by a carpenter and shoemaker if thou didst find fault because thou seest in their workshop shavings and cuttings from the things which they make. And yet they have places into which they can throw these shavings and cuttings ; but the universal nature has no external space ; now the wondrous part of her art is that though she has circumscribed her-

self, everything within her which appears to decay
and to grow old and to be useless she changes into
herself, and again makes other new things from
these very same, so that she requires neither substance from without nor wants a place into which
she may cast that which decays. She is content
then with her own space, and her own matter and
her own art.

51. Neither in thy actions be sluggish nor in
thy conversation without method, nor wandering
in thy thoughts, nor let there be in thy soul in-
ward contention nor external effusion, nor in life
be so busy as to have no leisure.

Suppose that men kill thee, cut thee in pieces,
curse thee. What then can these things do to
prevent thy mind from remaining pure, wise, sober,
just? For instance, if a man should stand by a
limpid pure spring, and curse it, the spring never
ceases sending up potable water; and if he should
cast clay into it or filth, it will speedily disperse
them and wash them out, and will not be at all
polluted. How then shalt thou possess a per-
petual fountain [and not a mere well]? By
forming thyself hourly to freedom conjoined with
benevolence, simplicity, and modesty.

52. He who does not know what the world is,
does not know where he is. And he who does

not kno.. for what purpose the world exists, does
not know who he is, nor what the world is. But
he who has failed in any one of these things could
not even say for what purpose he exists himself.
What then dost thou think of him who [avoids or]
seeks the praise of those who applaud, of men who
know not either where they are or who they are.

53. Dost thou wish to be praised by a man who
curses himself thrice every hour? wouldst thou
wish to please a man who does not please himself?
Does a man please himself who repents of nearly
everything that he does?

54. No longer let thy breathing only act in
concert with the air which surrounds thee, but let
thy intelligence also now be in harmony with the
intelligence which embraces all things. For the
intelligent power is no less diffused in all parts and
pervades all things for him who is willing to draw
it to him than the aerial power for him who is able
to respire it.

55. Generally, wickedness does no harm at all
to the universe; and particularly, the wickedness
[of one man] does no harm to another. It is only
harmful to him who has it in his power to be released from it, as soon as he shall choose.

56. To my own free will the free will of my
neighbor is just as indifferent as his breath and

his flesh. For though we are made especially for the sake of one another, still the ruling power of each of us has its own office, for otherwise my neighbor's wickedness would be my harm, which god has not willed in order that my unhappiness may not depend on another.

57. The sun appears to be poured down, and in all directions indeed it is diffused, yet it is not effused. For this diffusion is extension: Accordingly its rays are called Extensions [ἀκτῖνες] because they are extended [ἀπὸ τοῦ ἐκτείνεσθαι].[5] But one may judge what kind of a thing a ray is, if he looks at the sun's light passing through a narrow opening into a darkened room, for it is extended in a right line, and as it were is divided when it meets with a solid body which stands in the way and intercepts the air beyond; but there the light remains fixed and does not glide or fall off. Such then ought to be the outpouring and diffusion of the understanding, and it should in no way be an effusion, but an extension, and it should make no violent or impetuous collision with the obstacles which are in its way; nor yet fall down, but be fixed and enlighten that which receives it. For a body will deprive itself of the illumination, if it does not admit it.

[5] A piece of bad etymology.

58. He who fears death either fears the loss of sensation or a different kind of sensation. But if thou shalt have no sensation, neither wilt thou feel any harm; and if thou shalt acquire another kind of sensation, thou wilt be a different kind of living being and thou wilt not cease to live.

59. Men exist for the sake of one another. Teach them then or bear with them.

60. In one way an arrow moves, in another way the mind. The mind indeed, both when it exercises caution and when it is employed about inquiry, moves straight onward not the less, and to its object.

61. Enter into every man's ruling faculty; and also let every other man enter into thine.

IX.

HE who acts unjustly acts impiously. For since the universal nature has made rational animals for the sake of one another to help one another according to their deserts, but in no way to injure one another, he who transgresses her will, is clearly guilty of impiety towards the highest divinity. And he too who lies is guilty of impiety to the same divinity; for the universal nature is the nature of all things that are; and all things that are have a relation to all things that come into existence. And further, this universal nature is named truth and is the prime cause of all things that are true. He then who lies intentionally is guilty of impiety inasmuch as he acts unjustly by deceiving; and he also who lies unintentionally, inasmuch as he is at variance with the universal nature, and inasmuch as he disturbs the order by fighting against the nature of the world; for he fights against it, who is moved of himself to that which is contrary to truth,

for he had received powers from nature through the
neglect of which he is not able now to distinguish
falsehood from truth. And indeed he who pursues
pleasure as good, and avoids pain as evil is guilty
of impiety. For of necessity such a man must
often find fault with the universal nature, alleging
that it assigns things to the bad and the good contrary to their deserts, because frequently the bad
are in the enjoyment of pleasure and possess the
things which procure pleasure, but the good have
pain for their share and the things which cause
pain. And further, he who is afraid of pain will
sometimes also be afraid of some of the things
which will happen in the world, and even this is
impiety. And he who pursues pleasure will not
abstain from injustice, and this is plainly impiety.
Now with respect to the things towards which the
universal nature is equally affected, — for it would
not have made both, unless it was equally affected
towards both, — towards these they who wish to
follow nature should be of the same mind with it,
and equally affected. With respect to pain then
and pleasure or death and life or honor and dishonor, which the universal nature employs equally,
whoever is not equally affected is manifestly acting
impiously. And I say that the universal nature
employs them equally, instead of saying that they

happen alike to those who are produced in continuous series and to those who come after them
by virtue of a certain original movement of providence, according to which it moved from a certain
beginning to this ordering of things, having conceived certain reasons of the things which were to
be, and having determined generative powers of
substances and changes and such like succes-
sions.

2. It would be a man's happiest lot to depart
from mankind without having had any taste of
lying and hypocrisy and luxury and pride. However to breathe out one's life when a man has had
enough of these things is the next best voyage, as
the saying is. Hast thou determined to abide
with vice, and has not experience yet induced
thee to fly from this pestilence? For the destruction of the understanding is a pestilence,
much more indeed than any such corruption and
change of this atmosphere which surrounds us.
For this corruption is a pestilence of animals in
so far as they are animals; but the other is a
pestilence of men in so far as they are men.

3. Do not despise death, but be well content
with it, since this too is one of those things which
nature wills. For such as it is to be young and
to grow old, and to increase and to reach maturity,

and to have teeth and beard and gray hairs, and
to beget and to be pregnant and to bring forth,
and all the other natural operations which the
seasons of thy life bring, such also is dissolution.
This then is consistent with the character of a
reflecting man to be neither careless nor impa-
tient nor contemptuous with respect to death, but
to wait for it as one of the operations of nature.
As thou now waitest for the time when the child
shall come out of thy wife's womb, so be ready
for the time when thy soul shall fall out of this
envelope. But if thou requirest also a vulgar
kind of comfort which shall reach thy heart, thou
wilt be made best reconciled to death by observing the objects from which thou art going to be
removed and the morals of those with whom thy
soul will no longer be mingled. For it is no way
right to be offended with men, but it is thy duty
to care for them and to bear with them gently;
and yet to remember that thy departure will be
not from men who have the same principles as
thyself. For this is the only thing, if there be
any, which could draw us the contrary way and
attach us to life, to be permitted to live with
those who have the same principles as ourselves.
. But now thou seest how great is the trouble
arising from the discordance of those who live

together, so that thou mayst say, Come quick, O death, lest perchance I too should forget myself.

4. He who does wrong does wrong against himself. He who acts unjustly acts unjustly to himself, because he makes himself bad.

5. He often acts unjustly who does not do a certain thing; not only he who does a certain thing.

6. Thy present opinion founded on understanding, and thy present conduct directed to social good, and thy present disposition of contentment with everything which happens †— that is enough.

7. Wipe out imagination: check desire: extinguish appetite: keep the ruling faculty in its own power.

8. Among the animals which have not reason one life is distributed; but among reasonable animals one intelligent soul is distributed: just as there is one earth of all things which are of an earthy nature, and we see by one light, and breathe one air, all of us that have the faculty of vision and all that have life.

9. All things which participate in anything which is common to them all move towards that which is of the same kind with themselves. Everything which is earthy turns towards the earth, · everything which is liquid flows together, and

everything which is of an aerial kind does the same, so that they require something to keep them asunder and the application of force. Fire indeed moves upwards on account of the elemental fire, but it is so ready to be kindled together with all the fire which is here, that even every substance which is somewhat dry, is easily ignited, because there is less mingled with it of that which is a hindrance to ignition. Accordingly then everything also which participates in the common intelligent nature moves in like manner towards that which is of the same kind with itself, or moves even more. For so much as it is superior in comparison with all other things, in the same degree also is it more ready to mingle with and to be fused with that which is akin to it. Accordingly among animals devoid of reason we find swarms of bees, and herds of cattle, and the nurture of young birds, and in a manner, loves; for even in animals there are souls, and that power which brings them together is seen to exert itself in the superior degree, and in such a way as never has been observed in plants nor in stones nor in trees. But in rational animals there are political communities and friendships, and families and meetings of people; and in wars treaties and armistices. But in the things which

are still superior, even though they are separated
from one another, unity in a manner exists, as in
the stars. Thus the ascent to the higher degree
is able to produce a sympathy even in things
which are separated. See then what now takes
place. For only intelligent animals have now
forgotten this mutual desire and inclination,
and in them alone the property of flowing together is not seen. But still though men strive
to avoid [this union], they are caught and held
by it, for their nature is too strong for them; and
thou wilt see what I say, if thou only observest.
Sooner then will one find anything earthy which
comes in contact with no earthy thing than a
man altogether separated from other men.

10. Both man and god and the universe produce fruit; at the proper seasons each produces
it. But if usage has especially fixed these terms
to the vine and like things, this is nothing. Reason produces fruit both for all and for itself, and
there are produced from it other things of the
same kind as reason itself.

11. If thou art able, correct by teaching those
who do wrong; but if thou canst not, remember
that indulgence is given to thee for this purpose.
And the gods too are indulgent to such persons;
and for some purposes they even help them to get

health, wealth, reputation; so kind they are. And it is in thy power also; or say, who hinders thee?

12. Labor not as one who is wretched, nor yet as one who would be pitied or admired: but direct thy will to one thing only, to put thyself in motion and to check thyself, as the social reason requires.

13. To-day I have got out of all trouble, or rather I have cast out all trouble, for it was not outside, but within and in my opinions.

14. All things are the same, familiar in experience, and ephemeral in time, and worthless in the matter. Everything now is just as it was in the time of those whom we have buried.

15. Things stand outside of us, themselves by themselves, neither knowing aught of themselves, nor expressing any judgment. What is it then which does judge about them? The ruling faculty.

16. Not in passivity, but in activity lie the evil and the good of the rational social animal, just as his virtue and his vice lie not in passivity, but in activity.

17. For the stone which has been thrown up it is no evil to come down, nor indeed any good to have been carried up. (VIII. 20.)

18. Penetrate inwards into men's leading principles, and thou wilt see what judges thou art afraid of, and what kind of judges they are of themselves.

19. All things are changing: and thou thyself art in continuous mutation and in a manner in continuous destruction, and the universe too.

20. It is thy duty to leave another man's wrongful act there where it is. (vii. 29, ix. 38.)

21. Termination of activity, cessation from movement and opinion, and in a sense their death, is no evil. Turn thy thoughts now to the consideration of thy life, thy life as a child, as a youth, thy manhood, thy old age, for in these also every change was a death. Is this anything to fear? Turn thy thoughts now to thy life under thy grandfather, then to thy life under thy mother, then to thy life under thy father; and as thou findest many other differences and changes and terminations, ask thyself, Is this anything to fear? In like manner then neither are the termination and cessation and change of thy whole life a thing to be afraid of?

22. Hasten [to examine] thy own ruling faculty and that of the universe and that of thy neighbor: thy own that thou mayst make it just: and that of the universe, that thou mayst

remember of what thou art a part; and that of thy neighbor, that thou mayst know whether he has acted ignorantly or with knowledge, and that thou mayst also consider that his ruling faculty is akin to thine.

23. As thou thyself art a component part of a social system, so let every act of thine be a component part of social life. Whatever act of thine then has no reference either immediately or remotely to a social end, this tears asunder thy life and does not allow· it to be one, and it is of the nature of a mutiny, just as when in a popular assembly a man acting by himself stands apart from the general agreement.

24. Quarrels of little children and their sports, and poor spirits carrying about dead bodies [such is everything] ; and so what is exhibited in the representation of the mansions of the dead [1] strikes our eyes more clearly.

25. Examine into the quality of the form of an object, and detach it altogether from its material part and then contemplate it ; then determine the time, the longest which a thing of this peculiar form is naturally made to endure.

[1] τὸ τῆς Νεκυίας may be, as Gataker conjectures, a dramatic representation of the state of the dead. Schulze supposes that it may be also a reference to the Νέκυια of the Odyssey (lib. xi.)

26. Thou hast endured infinite troubles through not being contented with thy ruling faculty, when it does the things which it is constituted by nature to do. But enough [of this].

27. When another blames thee or hates thee, or when men say about thee anything injurious, approach their souls, penetrate within, and see what kind of men they are. Thou wilt discover that there is no reason to take any trouble that these men may have this or that opinion about thee. However thou must be well disposed towards them, for by nature they are friends. And the gods too aid them in all ways, by dreams, by signs, towards the attainment of those things on which they set a value.

28. The periodic movements of the universe are the same, up and down from age to age. And either the universal intelligence puts itself in motion for every separate effect, and if this is so, be thou content with that which is the result of its activity; or it put itself in motion once, and everything else comes by way of sequence [2] in a manner: or indivisible elements are the origin of all things.—In a word, if there is a god,

[2] The words which immediately follow κατ' ἐπακολού-θησιν are corrupt. But the meaning is hardly doubtful. (Compare VII. 75.)

all is well; and if chance rules, do not thou also
be governed by it.

Soon will the earth cover us all :. then the earth
too will change, and the things also which result
from change will continue to change forever, and
these again forever. For if a man reflects on the
changes and transformations which follow one
another like wave after wave and their rapidity,
he will despise everything which is perishable.

29. The universal cause is like a winter torrent:
it carries everything along with it. But how
worthless are all these poor people who are engaged in matters political, and, as they suppose,
are playing the philosopher! All drivellers.
Well then, man : do what nature now requires.
Set thyself in motion, if it is in thy power, and
do not look about thee to see if any one will
observe it ; nor yet expect Plato's Republic : but
be content if the smallest thing goes on well, and
consider such an event to be no small matter.
For who can change men's principles? and without a change of principles what else is there than
the slavery of men who groan while they pretend
to obey? Come now and tell me of Alexander and Philippus and Demetrius of Phalerum.
They themselves shall judge whether they discovered what the universal nature required and

trained themselves accordingly. But if they acted like tragedy heroes, no one has condemned me to imitate them. Simple and modest is the work of philosophy. Draw me not aside to insolence and pride.

30. Look down from above on the countless herds of men and their countless solemnities, and the infinitely varied voyagings in storms and calms, and the differences among those who are born, who live together, and die. And consider too the life lived by others in olden time, and the life of those who will live after thee, and the life now lived among barbarous nations, and how many know not even thy name, and how many will soon forget it, and how they who perhaps now are praising thee will very soon blame thee, and that neither a posthumous name is of any value, nor reputation, nor anything else.

31. Let there be freedom from perturbations with respect to the things which come from the external cause; and let there be justice in the things done by virtue of the internal cause, that is, let there be movement and action terminating in this, in social acts, for this is according to thy nature.

32. Thou canst remove out of the way many useless things among those which disturb thee,

for they lie entirely in thy opinion ; and thou
wilt then gain for thyself ample space by com-
prehending the whole universe in thy mind and
by contemplating the eternity of time and observing the rapid change of every several thing, how
short is the time from its birth to its dissolution,
and the illimitable time before its birth as well as
the equally boundless time after its dissolution.

33. All that thou seest will quickly perish,
and those who have been spectators of its dissolution will very soon perish too. And he who
dies at the extremest old age will be brought
into the same condition with him who died pre-
maturely.

34. What are these men's leading principles,
and about what kind of things are they busy, and
for what kind of reasons do they love and honor
Imagine that thou seest their poor souls laid bare.
When they think that they do harm by their
blame or good by their praise, what an idea !

35. Loss is nothing else than change. But the
universal nature delights in change, and in
obedience to her all things are now done well, and
from eternity have been done in like form, and
will be such to time without end. What then dost
thou say ? That all things have been and all
things always will be bad, and that no power has

ever been found in so many gods to rectify these things, but the world has been condemned to be bound in never ceasing evil?

36. The rottenness of the matter which is the substance of everything! water, dust, bones, filth: or again, marble rocks, the callosities of the earth; and gold and silver, the sediments; and garments, only bits of hair; and purple dye, blood; and everything else is of the same kind. And that which is of the nature of breath is also another thing of the same kind, changing from this to that.

37. Enough of this wretched life and murmuring and apish tricks. Why art thou disturbed? What is there new in this? What unsettles thee? Is it the form of the thing? Look at it. Or is it the matter? Look at it. But besides these there is nothing. Towards the gods then now become at last more simple and better. It is the same whether we look at these things for a hundred years or three.

38. If any man has done wrong, the harm is his own. But perhaps he has not done wrong.

39. Either all things proceed from one intelligent source and come together as in one body, and the part ought not to find fault with what is done for the benefit of the whole: or there are only

atoms and nothing else than mixture and dispersion. Why then art thou disturbed? Say to the ruling faculty, Art thou dead, art thou corrupted, art thou playing the hypocrite, art thou become a beast, dost thou herd and feed with the rest?[3]

40. Either the gods have no power or they have power. If then they have no power, why dost thou pray to them? But if they have power, why dost thou not pray for them to give thee the faculty of not fearing any of the things which thou fearest, or of not desiring any of the things which thou desirest, or not being pained at anything, rather than pray that any of these things should not happen or happen? for certainly if they can co-operate with men, they can co-operate for these purposes. But perhaps thou wilt say, the gods have placed them in thy power. Well then, is it not better to use what is in thy power like a free man, than to desire in a slavish and abject way what is not in thy power? And who has told thee that the gods do not aid us even in the things which are in our power? Begin

---

[3] There is some corruption at the end of this section. I believe that the translation expresses the emperor's meaning. Whether intelligence rules all things or chance rules, a man must not be disturbed. He must use the power that he has, and be tranquil.

then to pray for such things and thou wilt see.
One man prays thus: How shall I be able to lie
with that woman? Do thou pray thus: How
shall I not desire to lie with her? Another prays
thus, How shall I be released from this? Another
prays: How shall I not desire to be released?
Another thus, How shall I not lose my little son?
Thou thus, How shall I not be afraid to lose him.
In fine, turn thy prayers this way, and see what
comes.

41. Epicurus says, In my sickness my conversation was not about my bodily sufferings, nor, says
he, did I talk on such subjects to those who visited
me; but I continued to discourse on the nature of
things as before, keeping to this main point, how
the mind while participating in such movements
as go on in the poor flesh shall be free from perturbations and maintain its proper good. Nor did
I, he says, give the physicians an opportunity of
putting on solemn looks, as if they were doing
something great, but my life went on well and
happily. Do then the same that he did both in
sickness, if thou art sick, and in any other circumstances; for never to desert philosophy in any
events that may befall us, nor to hold trifling talk
either with an ignorant man or with one unac-
quainted with nature, is a principle of all schools

of philosophy ; but to be intent only on that which
thou art now doing and on the instrument by
which thou doest it.

42. When thou art offended with any man's
shameless conduct, immediately ask thyself, Is it
possible then that shameless men should not be in
the world? It is not possible. Do not then require
what is impossible. For this man also is one of
those shameless men, who must of necessity be in
the world. Let the same considerations be present
to thy mind in the case of the knave, and the
faithless man, and of every man who does wrong
in any way. For at the same time that thou dost
remind thyself that it is impossible that such kind
of men should not exist, thou wilt become better
disposed towards every one individually. It is useful to perceive this too immediately when the occasion arises, what virtue nature has given to man to
oppose to every wrongful act. For she has given
to man as an antidote, against the stupid man
mildness, and against another kind of man some
other power. And in all cases it is possible for
thee to correct by teaching the man who is gone
astray ; for every man who errs misses his object
and is gone astray. Besides wherein hast thou
been injured? For thou wilt find that no one
among those against whom thou art irritated has

done anything by which thy mind could be made worse ; but that which is evil to thee and harmful has its foundation only in the mind. And what harm is done or what is there strange, if the man who has not been instructed does the acts of an uninstructed man? Consider whether thou shouldst not rather blame thyself, because thou didst not expect such a man to err in such a way. For thou hadst means given thee by thy reason to suppose that it was likely that he would commit this error, and yet thou hast forgotten and art amazed that he has erred. But most of all when thou blamest a man as faithless or ungrateful, turn to thyself. For the fault is manifestly thy own, whether thou- didst trust that a man who had such a disposition would keep his promise, or when conferring thy kindness thou didst not confer it absolutely, nor yet in such way as to have received from thy very act all the profit. For what more dost thou want when thou hast done a man a service ? art thou not content that thou hast done something conformable to thy nature, and dost thou seek to be paid for it? just as if the eye demanded a recompense for seeing, or the feet for walking. For as these members are formed for a particular purpose, and by working according to their several constitutions obtain what is their own ; so also as man is formed

by nature to acts of benevolence, when he has
done anything benevolent or in any other way
conducive to the common interest, he has acted
conformably to his constitution and he gets what
is his own.

X.

ILT thou then, my soul, never be good and simple and one and naked, more manifest than the body which surrounds thee? Wilt thou never enjoy an affectionate and contented disposition? Wilt thou never be full and without a want of any kind, longing for nothing more, nor desiring anything either animate or inanimate for the enjoyment of pleasures? nor yet desiring time wherein thou shalt have longer enjoyment, or place, or pleasant climate, or society of men with whom thou mayst live in harmony? but wilt thou be satisfied with thy present condition, and pleased with all that is about thee, and wilt thou convince thyself that thou hast everything and that it comes from the gods, that everything is well for thee and will be well whatever shall please them. and whatever they shall give for the conservation of the perfect living being, the good and just and beautiful, which generates and holds together all

things, and contains and embraces all things which
are dissolved for the production of other like
things? Wilt thou never be such that thou shalt
so dwell in community with gods and men as'
neither to find fault with them at all nor to be
condemned by them?

2. Observe what thy nature requires, so far as
thou art governed by nature only : then do it and
accept it, if thy nature, so far as thou art a living
being shall not be made worse by it. And next
thou must observe what thy nature requires so far
as thou art a living being. And all this thou
mayst allow thyself, if thy nature, so far as thou
art a rational animal, shall not be made worse by
it. But the rational animal is consequently also
a political [social] animal. Use these rules then
and trouble thyself about nothing else.

3. Everything which happens either happens in
such wise that thou art formed by nature to bear
it, or that thou art not formed by nature to bear
it. If then it happens to thee in such way that
thou art formed by nature to bear it, do not complain, but bear it as thou art formed by nature to
bear it. But if it happens in such wise that thou
art not able to bear it, do not complain, for it will
perish after it has consumed thee. Remember
however that thou art formed by nature to bear

everything, with respect to which it depends on
thy own opinion to make it endurable and tolerable, by thinking that it is either thy interest or
thy duty to do this.

4. If a man is mistaken, instruct him kindly
and show him his error. But if thou art not able,
blame thyself, or blame not even thyself.

5. Whatever may happen to thee, it was prepared for thee from all eternity; and the impli-
cation of causes was from eternity spinning the
thread of thy being and of that which is incident
to it. (III. 11; IV. 26.)

6. Whether the universe is [a concourse of]
atoms, or nature [is a system], let this first be
established, that I am a part of the whole which
is governed by nature; next, I am in a manner
intimately related to the parts which are of the
same kind with myself. For remembering this,
inasmuch as I am a part, I shall be discontented
with none of the things which are assigned to me
out of the whole; for nothing is injurious to the
part, if it is for the advantage of the whole. For
the whole contains nothing which is not for its
advantage; and all natures indeed have this common principle, but the nature of the universe has
this principle besides, that it cannot be compelled
even by any external cause to generate anything

harmful to itself. By remembering then that I
am a part of such a whole, I shall be content with
everything that happens. And inasmuch as I am
in a manner intimately related to the parts which
are of the same kind with myself, I shall do
nothing unsocial, but I shall rather direct myself
to the things which are of the same kind with
myself, and I shall turn all my efforts to the common interest, and divert them from the contrary.
Now if these things are done so, life must flow on
happily, just as thou mayst observe that the life of
a citizen is happy, who continues a course of action
which is advantageous to his fellow-citizens, and is
content with whatever the state may assign to him.

7. The parts of the whole, everything I mean
which is naturally comprehended in the universe,
must of necessity perish ; but let this be understood
in this sense, that they must undergo change.
But if this is naturally both an evil and a necessity
for the parts, the whole would not continue to
exist in a good condition, the parts being subject
to change and constituted so as to perish in various
ways. For whether did nature herself design to
do evil to the things which are parts of herself,
and to make them subject to evil and of necessity
fall into evil. or have such results happened with-

out her knowing it? Both these suppositions indeed are incredible. But if a man should even
drop the term Nature [as an efficient power] and
should speak of these things [change] as natural,
even then it would be ridiculous to affirm at the
same time that the parts of the whole are in their
nature subject to change, and at the same time to
be surprised or vexed as if something were hap-
pening contrary to nature, particularly as the dis-
solu ion of things is into those things of which each
thing is composed. For there is either a dispersion of the elements out of which everything has
been compounded, or a change from the solid to
the earthy and from the airy to the aerial, so that
these parts are taken back into the universal reason, whether this at certain periods is consumed by
fire or renewed by eternal changes. And do not
imagine that the solid and the airy part belong to
thee from the time of generation. For all this
received its accretion only yesterday and the day
before, as one may say, from the food and the air
which is inspired. This then, which has received
[the accretion], changes, not that which thy mother brought forth. But suppose that this [which
thy mother brought forth] implicates thee very
much with that other part, which has the peculiar

quality [of change], this is nothing in fact in the
way of objection to what is said.[1]

8. When thou hast assumed these names, good,
modest, true, rational, a man of equanimity, and
magnanimous, take care that thou dost not change
these names ; and if thou shouldst lose them,
quickly return to them. And remember that the
term Rational was intended to signify a discrimi-
nating attention to every several thing and freedom
from negligence ; and that Equanimity is the
voluntary acceptance of the things which are assigned to thee by the common nature ; and that
Magnanimity is the elevation of the intelligent part
above the pleasurable or painful sensations of the
flesh and above that poor thing called fame, and
death, and all such things. If then thou main-
tainest thyself in the possession of these names,
without desiring to be called by these names by
others, thou wilt be another person and wilt enter
on another life. For to continue to be such as thou
hast hitherto been, and to be torn in pieces and
defiled in such a life, is the character of a very
stupid man and one overfond of his life, and like
those half-devoured fighters with wild beasts, who

[1] The end of this section is perhaps corrupt. The
meaning is very obscure. I have given that meaning
which appears to be consistent with the whole argument.

though covered with wounds and gore, still intreat to be kept to the following day, though they will be exposed in the same state to the same claws and bites. Therefore fix thyself in the possession of these few names : and if thou art able to abide in them, abide as if thou wast removed to certain islands of the Happy.[2] But if thou shalt perceive that thou fallest out of them and dost not maintain thy hold, go courageously into some nook where

[2] The islands of the Happy or the Fortunatae Insulae are spoken of by the Greek and Roman writers. They were the abode of Heroes, like Achilles and Diomedes, as we see in the Scolion of Harmodius and Aristogiton. Sertorius heard of the islands at Cadiz from some sailors who had been there, and he had a wish to go and live in them and rest from his troubles. (Plutarch, Sertorius, c. 8.) In the Odyssey, Proteus told Menelaus that he should not die in Argos, but be removed to a place at the boundary of the earth where Rhadamanthus dwelt: (Odyssey, IV. 565.)

> For there in sooth man's life is easiest .
> Nor snow nor raging storm nor rain is there,
> But ever gently breathing gales of Zephyr
> Oceanus sends up to gladden man.

It is certain that the writer of the Odyssey only follows some old legend without having any knowledge of any place which corresponds to his description. The two islands which Sertorius heard of may be Madeira and the adjacent island.

thou shalt maintain them, or even depart at once
from life, not in passion, but with simplicity and
freedom and modesty, after doing this one [laud-
able] thing at least in thy life, to have gone out
of it thus. In order however to the remembrance
of these names, it will greatly help thee, if thou
rememberest the gods and that they wish not to
be flattered, but wish all reasonable beings to be
made like themselves; and if thou rememberest
that what does the work of a fig-tree is a fig-tree,
and that what does the work of a dog is a dog,
and that what does the work of a bee is a bee,
and that what does the work of a man is a man.

9. Mimi,[3] war, astonishment, torpor, slavery,
will daily wipe out those holy principles of thine.
† How many things without studying nature dost
thou imagine and how many dost thou neglect?[4]
But it is thy duty so to look on and so to do
everything, that at the same time the power of
dealing with circumstances is perfected, and the
contemplative faculty is exercised, and the confidence which comes from the knowledge of each
several thing is maintained without showing it,

---

[3] Corae conjectured μῖσος "hatred" in place of Mimi,
Roman plays in which action and gesticulation were all
or nearly all.

[4] This is corrupt.

but yet not concealed. For when wilt thou enjoy simplicity, when gravity, and when the knowledge of every several thing, both what it is in substance, and what place it has in the universe, and how long it is formed to exist and of what things it is compounded, and to whom it can belong, and who are able both to give it and take it away?

10. A spider is proud when it has caught a fly, and another when he has caught a poor hare, and another when he has taken a little fish in a net, and another when he has taken wild boars, and another when he has taken bears, and another when he has taken Sarmatians. Are not these robbers, if thou examinest their principles? [5]

11. Acquire the contemplative way of seeing how all things change into one another, and constantly attend to it, and exercise thyself about this part [of philosophy]. For nothing is so much adapted to produce magnanimity. Such a man has put off the body, and as he sees that he must, no one knows how soon, go away from among men and leave everything here, he gives himself up entirely to just doing in all his actions, and in everything else that happens he resigns himself

[5] Marcus means to say that conquerors are robbers. He himself warred against Sarmatians, and was a robber, as he says, like the rest.

to the universal nature. But as to what any man shall say or think about him or do against him, he never even thinks of it, being himself contented with these two things, with acting justly in what he now does, and being satisfied with what is now assigned to him; and he lays aside all distracting and busy pursuits and desires nothing else than to accomplish the straight course through the law,[6] and by accomplishing the straight course to follow god.

12. What need is there of suspicious fear, since it is in thy power to inquire what ought to be done? And if thou seest clear, go by this way content, without turning back : but if thou dost not see clear, stop and take the best advisers. But if any other things oppose thee, go on according to thy powers with due consideration, keeping to that which appears to be just. For it is best to reach this object, and if thou dost fail, let thy failure be in attempting this. He who follows reason in all things is both tranquil and active at the same time, and also cheerful and collected.

13. Inquire of thyself as soon as thou wakest from sleep, whether it will make any difference to

---

[6] By the law, he means the divine law, obedience to the will of God.

thee, if another does what is just and right. It will make no difference.

Hast thou forgotten that those who assume arrogant airs in bestowing their praise or blame on others, are such as they are at bed and at board, and hast thou forgotten what they do, and what they avoid and what they pursue, and how they steal and how they rob, not with hands and feet, but with their most valuable part, by means of which there is produced, when a man chooses, fidelity, modesty, truth, law, a good daemon [happiness]? (VII. 17.)

14. To her who gives and takes back all, to nature, the man who is instructed and modest says: Give what thou wilt; take back what thou wilt. And he says this not proudly, but obediently and well pleased with her.

15. Short is the little which remains to thee of life. Live as on a mountain. For it makes no difference whether a man lives there or here, if he lives everywhere in the world as in a state [political community]. Let men see, let them know a real man who lives according to nature. If they cannot endure him, let them kill him. For that is better than to live thus [as men do].

16. No longer talk about the kind of man that a good man ought to be, but be such.

17. Constantly contemplate the whole of time and the whole of substance, and consider that all individual things as to substance are a grain of a fig, and as to time, the turning of a gimlet.

18. Look at everything that exists and observe that it is already in dissolution and in change and as it were putrefaction or dispersion, or that everything is so constituted by nature as to die.

19. Consider what men are when they are eating, sleeping, generating, easing themselves and so forth. Then what kind of men they are when they are imperious † and arrogant, or angry and scolding from their elevated place. But a short time ago to how many they were slaves and for what things; and after a little time consider in what a condition they will be.

20. That is for the good of each thing, which the universal nature brings to each. And it is for its good at the time when nature brings it.

21. " The earth loves the shower ;." and " the solemn aether loves :" and the universe loves to make whatever is about to be. I say then to the universe, that I love as thou lovest. And is not this too said, that " this or that loves [is wont] to be produced ? " [7]

[7] These words are from Euripides. They are cited by Aristotle, Ethic. Nicom. viii. 1. Athenaeus (xiii.

22. Either thou livest here and hast already accustomed thyself to it, or thou art going away, and this was thy own will; or thou art dying and hast discharged thy duty. But besides these things there is nothing. Be of good cheer then.

23. Let this always be plain to thee, that this piece of land is like any other; and that all things here are the same with things on the top of a mountain, or on the sea-shore, or wherever thou choosest to be. For thou wilt find just what Plato says, Making the walls of the city like a shepherd's fold on a mountain. [The three last words are omitted. They are unintelligible.] [8]

24. What is my ruling faculty now to me? and of what nature am I now making it? and for what purpose am I now using it? is it void of under-

296.) and Stobaeus quote seven complete lines beginning ἐρᾷ μὲν ὄμβρου γαῖα. There is a similar fragment of Aeschylus.

It was the fashion of the Stoics to work on the meanings of words. So Antoninus here takes the verb φιλεῖ, "loves," which has also the sense of "is wont," "uses," and the like. He finds in the common language of mankind a philosophical truth, and most great truths are expressed in the common language of life; some understand them, but most people express them without knowing how much they mean.

[8] Plato, Theaet. 174 D. E.

standing? is it loosed and rent asunder from social life? is it melted into and mixed with the poor flesh so as to move together with it?

25. He who flies from his master is a runaway; but the law is master, and he who breaks the law is a runaway. And he also who is grieved or angry or afraid,† is dissatisfied because something has been or is or shall be of the things which are appointed by him who rules all things, and he is Law, and assigns to every man what is fit. He then who fears or is grieved or is angry is a runaway.[9]

26. A man deposits seed in a womb and goes away, and then another cause takes it, and labors on it and makes a child. What a thing from such a material! Again, the child passes food down through the throat, and then another cause takes it and makes perception and motion, and in fine life and strength and other things ; how many and how strange ! Observe then the things which are produced in such a hidden way, and see the power just as we see the power which carries things downwards and upwards, not with the eyes, but still no less plainly.

---

[9] Antoninus is here playing on the etymology of νόμος, law, assignment, that which assigns (νέμει) to every man his portion.

27. Constantly consider how all things such as they now are, in time past also were; and consider that they will be the same again. And place before thy eyes entire dramas and stages of the same form, whatever thou hast learned from thy experience or from older history; for example the whole court of Hadrianus, and the whole court of Antoninus, and the whole court of Philippus, Alexander, Croesus; for all those were such dramas as we see now, only with different actors.

28. Imagine every man who is grieved at anything or discontented to be like a pig which is sacrificed, and kicks and screams.

Like this pig also is he who on his bed in silence laments the bonds in which we are held. And consider that only to the rational animal is it given to follow voluntarily what happens; but simply to follow is a necessity imposed on all.

29. Severally on the occasion of everything that thou doest pause and ask thyself, if death is a dreadful thing because it deprives thee of this.

30. When thou art offended at any man's fault, forthwith turn to thyself and reflect in what like manner thou dost err thyself; for example, in thinking that money is a good thing, or pleasure, or reputation and the like. For by attending to this thou wilt quickly forget thy anger, if this

consideration also is added, that the man is compelled : for what else could he do? or, if thou art able, take away from him the compulsion.

31. When thou hast seen Satyron the Socratic,† think of either Eutyches or Hymen, and when thou hast seen Euphrates, think of Eutychion or Silvanus, and when thou hast seen Alciphron think of Tropaeophorus, and when thou hast seen Xenophon think of Crito or Severus, and when thou hast looked on thyself, think of any other Caesar, and in the case of every one do in like manner. Then let this thought be in thy mind, Where then are those men? Nowhere, or nobody knows where. For thus continuously thou wilt look at human things as smoke and nothing at all ; especially if thou reflectest at the same time that what has once changed will never exist again in the infinite duration of time. But thou, in what a brief space of time is thy existence? And why art thou not content to pass through this short time in an orderly way? What matter and opportunity [for thy activity] art thou avoiding? For what else are all these things, except exercises for the reason, when it has viewed carefully and by examination into their nature the things which happen in life? Persevere then until thou shalt have made these things thy own, as the stomach

which is strengthened makes all things its own, as
the blazing fire makes flame and brightness out
of everything that is thrown into it.

32. Let it not be in any man's power to say
truly of thee that thou art not simple or that thou
art not good; but let him be a liar whoever shall
think anything of this kind about thee; and this
is altogether in thy power. For who is he that
shall hinder thee from being good and simple?
Do thou only determine to live no longer, unless
thou shalt be such. For neither does reason
allow [thee to live], if thou art not such.

33. What is that which as to this material [our
life] can be done or said in the way most conformable to reason? For whatever this may be,
it is in thy power to do it or to say it; and do not
make excuses that thou art hindered. Thou wilt
not cease to lament till thy mind is in such a condition, that, what luxury is to those who enjoy
pleasure, such shall be to thee, in the matter which
is subjected and presented to thee, the doing of the
things which are conformable to man's constitution; for a man ought to consider as an enjoyment
everything which it is in his power to do according to his own nature. And it is in his power
everywhere. Now it is not given to a cylinder to
move everywhere by its own motion. nor yet to

water nor fire, nor to anything else which is governed by nature or an irrational soul, for the
things which check them and stand in the way
are many. But intelligence and reason are able
to go through everything that opposes them, and
in such manner as they are formed by nature
and as they choose. Place before thy eyes this
facility with which the reason will be carried
through all things, as fire upwards, as a stone
downwards, as a cylinder down an inclined sur-
face, and seek for nothing further. For all other
obstacles either affect the body only which is a
dead thing; or, except through opinion and the
yielding of the reason itself, they do not crush
nor do any harm of any kind; for if they did, he
who felt it would immediately become bad. Now
in the case of all things which have a certain
constitution, whatever harm may happen to any
of them, that which is so affected becomes consequently worse; but in the like case, a man becomes both better, if one may say so, and more
worthy of praise by making a right use of these
accidents. And finally remember that nothing
harms him who is really a citizen, which does not
harm the state; nor yet does anything harm the
state, which does not harm law [order]; and of
these things which are called misfortunes not one

harms law. What then does not harm law does
not harm either state or citizen.

34. To him who is penetrated by true principles even the briefest precept is sufficient, and any
common precept, to remind him that he should be
free from grief and fear.   For example —

> Leaves, some the wind scatters on the ground —
> So is the race of men.[10]

Leaves also are thy children; and leaves too are
they who cry out as if they were worthy of
credit and bestow their praise, or on the contrary curse, or secretly blame and sneer; and
leaves in like manner are those who shall receive
and transmit a man's fame to after times. For all
such things as these "are produced in the season
of spring," as the poet says; then the wind
casts them down; then the forest produces other
leaves in their places. But a brief existence is
common to all things, and yet thou avoidest and
pursuest all things as if they would be eternal.
A little time, and thou shalt close thy eyes; and
him who has attended thee to thy grave another
soon will lament.

35. The healthy eye ought to see all visible
things and not to say, I wish for green things;

1) Homer, Il. vi. 146.

for this is the condition of a diseased eye. And the healthy hearing and smelling ought to be ready to perceive all that can be heard and smelled. And the healthy stomach ought to be with respect to all food just as the mill with respect to all things which it is formed to grind. And accordingly the healthy understanding ought to be prepared for everything which happens; but that which says, Let my dear children live, and let all men praise whatever I may do, is an eye which seeks for green things, or teeth which seek for soft things.

36. There is no man so fortunate that there shall not be by him when he is dying some who are pleased with what is going to happen.[11] Suppose that he was a good and wise man, will there not be at last some one to say of him, Let us at last breathe freely being relieved from this schoolmaster. It is true that he was harsh to none of us, but I perceived that he tacitly condemns us. — This is what is said of a good man. But in our own case how many other things are there for which there are many who wish to get rid of us. Thou wilt consider this then when thou art dying,

---

[11] He says κακόν, but as he affirms in other places that death is no evil, he must mean what others may call an evil, and he means only "what is going to happen."

and thou wilt depart more contentedly by reflecting thus: I am going away from such a life, in
which even my associates in behalf of whom I
have striven so much, prayed, and cared, themselves wish me to depart, hoping perchance to get
some little advantage by it.   Why then should a
man cling to a longer stay here?   Do not however for this reason go away less kindly disposed
to them, but preserving thy own character, and
continuing friendly and benevolent and kind, and
on the other hand not as if thou wast torn away;
but as when a man dies a quiet death, the soul is
easily separated from the body, such also ought
thy departure from men to be, for nature united
thee to them and associated thee.   But does she
now dissolve the union?   Well, I am separated as
from kinsmen, not however dragged resisting, but
without compulsion; for this too is one of the
things according to nature.

37. Accustom thyself as much as possible on
the occasion of anything being done by any person to inquire with thyself, For what object is
this man doing this? but begin with thyself, and
examine thyself first.

38. Remember that this which pulls the strings
is the thing which is hidden within: this is the
power of persuasion, this is life, this, if one may

so say, is man. In contemplating thyself never include the vessel which surrounds thee and these instruments which are attached about it. For they are like to an axe, differing only in this that they grow to the body. For indeed there is no more use in these parts without the cause which moves and checks them, than in the weaver's shuttle, and the writer's pen and the driver's whip.[12]

[12] See " The Philosophy of Antoninus."

XI.

THESE are the properties of the rational soul: it sees itself, analyses itself, and makes itself such as it chooses; the fruit which it bears itself enjoys — for the fruits of plants and that in animals which corresponds to fruits others enjoy — it obtains its own end, wherever the limit of life may be fixed. Not as in a dance and in a play and in such like things, where the whole action is incomplete, if anything cuts it short; but in every part and wherever it may be stopped, it makes what has been set before it full and complete, so that it can say, I have what is my own. And further it traverses the whole universe, and the surrounding vacuum, and surveys its form, and it extends itself into the infinity of time and embraces and comprehends the periodical renovation of all things, and it comprehends that those who come after us will see nothing new, nor have those before us seen anything more, but in a manner he who is forty years old, if he has any understanding at all, has seen by virtue of the uniformity that prevails all things which have been and all that will be. This too is a property of the rational soul, love of one's neighbor, and truth and modesty, and to value nothing more than itself, which is also the property of Law.[1] Thus then right reason differs not at all from the reason of justice.

2. Thou wilt set little value on pleasing song and dancing and the pancratium, if thou wilt distribute the melody of the voice into its several sounds, and ask thyself as to each, if thou art mastered by this; for thou wilt be prevented by shame from confessing it: and in the matter of dancing, if at each movement and attitude thou wilt do the same; and the like also in the matter of the pancratium. In all things then, except virtue and the acts of virtue, remember to apply thyself to their several parts, and by this division to come to value them little: and apply this rule also to thy whole life.

3. What a soul that is which is ready, if at any moment it must be separated from the body, and ready either to be extinguished or dispersed or continue to exist; but so that this readiness

[1] Law is the order by which all things are governed.

comes from a man's own judgment, not from mere
obstinacy, as with the Christians, but considerately
and with dignity and in a way to persuade another, without tragic show.

4. Have I done something for the general interest? Well then I have had my reward. Let
this always be present to thy mind, and never
stop [doing good].

5. What is thy art? to be good. And how is
this accomplished well except by general principles, some about the nature of the universe, and
others about the proper constitution of man?

6. At first tragedies were brought on the stage
as means of reminding men of the things which
happen to them, and that it is according to nature
for things to happen so, and that, if thou art de-
lighted with what is shown on the stage, thou
shouldst not be troubled with that which takes
place on the larger stage. For thou seest that
these things must be accomplished thus, and that
even they bear them who cry out [2] "O Cithae-
ron." And indeed some things are said well by
the dramatic writers, of which kind is the following especially : —

> Me and my children if the gods neglect,
> This has its reason too.[3]

[2] Sophocles, Oedipus Rex.

[3] See VII. 41. 38. 40

And again

> We must not chafe and fret at that which happens.

And

> Life's harvest reap like the wheat's fruitful ear.

And other things of the same kind.

After tragedy the old comedy was introduced, which had a magisterial freedom of speech, and by its very plainness of speaking was useful in reminding men to beware of insolence ; and for this purpose too Diogenes used to take from these writers.

But as to the middle comedy which came next, observe what it was, and again, for what object the new comedy was introduced, which gradually sunk down into a mere mimic artifice. That some good things are said by these writers too, everybody knows : but the whole plan of such poetry and dramaturgy, to what end does it look !

7. How plain does it appear that there is not another condition of life so well suited for philosophizing as this in which thou now happenest to be.

8. A branch cut off from the adjacent branch must of necessity be cut off from the whole tree also. So too a man when he is separated from another man has fallen off from the whole social

18

community. Now as to a branch, another cuts it
off, but a man by his own act separates himself
from his neighbor when he hates him and turns
away from him, and he does not know that he
has at the same time cut himself off from the
whole social system. Yet he has this privilege
certainly from Zeus who framed society, for it is
in our power to grow again to that which is near
to us and again to become a part which helps to
make up the whole. However if it often happens,
this kind of separation, it makes it difficult for
that which detaches itself to be brought to unity
and to be restored to its former condition. Finally, the branch, which from the first grew together with the tree and has continued to have
one life with it, is not like that which after being
cut off is then ingrafted, but it is something like
what the gardeners mean when they say that it
grows with the rest of the tree, but † that it has
not the same mind with it.

9. As those who try to stand in thy way when
thou art proceeding according to right reason,
will not be able to turn thee aside from thy proper
action, so neither let them drive thee from thy
benevolent feelings towards them, but be on thy
guard equally in both matters, not only in the
matter of steady judgment and action, but also in

the matter of gentleness towards those who try to hinder or otherwise trouble thee. For this also is a weakness, to be vexed at them, as well as to be diverted from thy course of action and to give way through fear; for both are equally deserters from their post, the man who does it through fear. and the man who is alienated from him who is by nature a kinsman and a friend.

10. There is no nature which is inferior to art. for the arts imitate the natures of things. But it this is so. that nature which is the most perfect and the most comprehensive of all natures, cannot fall short of the skill of art. Now all arts do the inferior things for the sake of the superior; therefore the universal nature does so too. And indeed hence is the origin of justice, and in justice the other virtues have their foundation : for justice will not be observed, if we either care for middle things [things indifferent]. or are easily deceived and careless and changeable. (v. 16. 30 ; vii. 55.)

11. If the things do not come to thee, the pursuits and avoidances of which disturb thee, still in a manner thou goest to them. Let then thy judgment about them be at rest, and they will remain quiet, and thou wilt not be seen either pursuing or avoiding.

12. The spherical form of the soul maintains its figure, when it is neither extended towards any object, nor contracted inwards, nor dispersed nor sinks down, but is illuminated by light, by which it sees the truth, the truth of all things and the truth that is in itself. (VIII. 41. 45 ; XII. 3.)

13. Suppose any man shall despise me. Let him look to that himself. But I will look to this, that I be not discovered doing or saying anything deserving of contempt. Shall any man hate me? Let him look to it. But I will be mild and benevolent towards every man and even to him, ready to show him his mistake, not reproachfully, nor yet as making a display of my endurance, but nobly and honestly, like the great Phocion, unless indeed he only assumed it. For the interior [parts] ought to be such, and a man ought to be seen by the gods neither dissatisfied with anything nor complaining. For what evil is it to thee, if thou art now doing what is agreeable to thy own nature and art satisfied with that which at this moment is suitable to the nature of the universe, since thou art a human being placed at thy post †to endure whatever is for the common advantage?

14. Men despise one another and flatter one another ; and men wish to raise themselves above one another and crouch before one another.

15. How unsound and insincere is he who says, I have determined to deal with thee in a fair way. — What art thou doing, man? There is no occasion to give this notice. It will soon show itself by acts. The voice ought to be plainly written on the forehead. Such as a man's character is,† he immediately shows it in his eyes, just as he who is beloved forthwith reads everything in the eyes of lovers. The man who is honest and good ought to be exactly like a man who smells strong, so that the bystander as soon as he comes near him must smell whether he choose or not. But the affectation of simplicity is like a crooked stick.⁴ Nothing is more disgraceful than a wolfish friendship [false friendship]. Avoid this most of all. The good and simple and benevolent show all these things in the eyes, and there is no mistaking.

16. As to living in the best way, this power is in the soul, if it be indifferent to things which are indifferent. And it will be indifferent, if it looks on each of these things separately and all together,

---

⁴ Instead of σκάλμη Saumaise reads σκαμβή. There is a Greek proverb, σκαμβὸν ξύλον οὐδέποτ' ὀρθόν: "You cannot make a crooked stick straight."

The wolfish friendship is an allusion to the fable of the sheep and the wolves.

and if it remembers that not one of them produces in us an opinion about itself, nor comes to
us ; but these things remain immovable, and it is
we ourselves who produce the judgments about
them, and, as we may say, write them in ourselves,
it being in our power not to write them, and it
being in our power, if perchance these judgments
have imperceptibly got admission to our minds,
to wipe them out ; and if we remember also that
such attention will only be for a short time, and
then life will be at an end.   Besides what trouble
is there at all in doing this?   For if these things
are according to nature, rejoice in them, and they
will be easy to thee : but if contrary to nature,
seek what is conformable to thy own nature, and
strive towards this, even if it bring no reputation ;
for every man is allowed to seek his own good.

18. Consider whence each thing is come, and
of what it consists,† and into what it changes, and
what kind of a thing it will be when it has
changed, and that it will sustain no harm.

18. [If any have offended against thee, consider
first]: What is my relation to men, and that we
are made for one another; and in another respect,
I was made to be set over them, as a ram over the
flock or a bull over the herd.   But examine the
matter from first principles, from this: If all

things are not mere atoms, it is nature which
orders all things : if this is so, the inferior things
exist for the sake of the superior and these for
the sake of one another. (II. 1 ; IX. 39 ; v. 16 ;
III. 4.)

Second, consider what kind of men they are
at table, in bed, and so forth : and particularly,
under what compulsions in respect of opinions
they are; and as to their acts, consider with what
pride they do what they do. (VIII. 14 ; IX. 34.)

Third, that if men do rightly what they do, we
ought not to be displeased; but if they do not
right, it is plain that they do so involuntarily and
in ignorance. For as every soul is unwillingly
deprived of the truth, so also is it unwillingly
deprived of the power of behaving to each man
according to his deserts. Accordingly men are
pained when they are called unjust, ungrateful,
and greedy, and in a word wrongdoers to their
neighbors. (VII. 62, 63 ; II. 1 ; VII. 26 ; VIII. 29.)

Fourth, consider that thou also doest many
things wrong, and that thou art a man like others ; and even if thou dost abstain from certain
faults, still thou hast the disposition to commit
them, though either through cowardice, or concern about reputation or some such mean motive,
thou dost abstain from such faults. (I. 17.)

Fifth, consider that thou dost not even understand whether men are doing wrong or not, for many things are done with a certain reference to circumstances. And in short, a man must learn a great deal to enable him to pass a correct judgment on another man's acts. (IX. 38 ; IV. 51.)

Sixth, consider when thou art much vexed or grieved, that man's life is only a moment, and after a short time we are all laid out dead. (VII. 58 ; IV. 48.)

Seventh, that it is not men's acts which disturb us, for those acts have their foundation in men's ruling principles, but it is our own opinions which disturb us. Take away these opinions then, and resolve to dismiss thy judgment about an act as if it were something grievous, and thy anger is gone. How then shalt thou take away these opinions ? By reflecting that no wrongful act of another brings shame on thee : for unless that which is shameful is alone bad, thou also must of necessity do many things wrong and become a robber and everything else. (V. 25 ; VII. 16.)

Eighth, consider how much more pain is brought on us by the anger and vexation caused by such acts than by the acts themselves, at which we are angry and vexed. (IV. 39. 49 ; VII. 24.)

Ninth, consider that benevolence is invincible, if it be genuine, and not an affected smile and acting a part. For what will the most violent man do to thee, if thou continuest to be of a benevolent disposition towards him, and if, as opportunity offers, thou gently admonishest him and calmly correctest his errors at the very time when he is trying to do thee harm, saying, Not so, my child: we are constituted by nature for something else: I shall certainly not be injured, but thou art injuring thyself, my child. — And show him with gentle tact and by general principles that this is so, and that even bees do not do as he does, nor any animals which are formed by nature to be gregarious. And thou must do this neither with any double meaning nor in the way of reproach, but affectionately and without any rancour in thy soul; and not as if thou wert lecturing him, nor yet that any bystander may admire, but either when he is alone, and if others are present . . .[5]

Remember these nine rules, as if thou hadst received them as a gift from the Muses, and begin at last to be a man, so long as thou livest. But thou must equally avoid flattering men and being vexed at them, for both are unsocial and

[5] It appears that there is a defect in the text here.

lead to harm. And let this truth be present to thee in the excitement of anger, that to be moved by passion is not manly, but that mildness and gentleness, as they are more agreeable to human nature, so also are they more manly; and he who possesses these qualities possesses strength, nerves, and courage, and not the man who is subject to fits of passion and discontent. For in the same degree in which a man's mind is nearer to freedom from all passion, in the same degree also is it nearer to strength: and as the sense of pain is a characteristic of weakness, so also is anger. For he who yields to pain and he who yields to anger, both are wounded and both submit. But if thou wilt, receive also a tenth present from the leader of the Muses [Apollo], and it is this — that to expect bad men not to do wrong is madness, for he who expects this desires an impossibility. But to allow men to behave so to others, and to expect them not to do thee any wrong, is irrational and tyrannical.

19. There are four principal aberrations of the superior faculty against which thou shouldst be constantly on thy guard, and when thou hast detected them, thou shouldst wipe them out and say on each occasion thus: this thought is not necessary: this tends to destroy social union:

this which thou art going to say comes not from
the real thoughts; for thou shouldst consider it
among the most absurd of things for a man not
to speak from his real thoughts. But the fourth
is when thou shalt reproach† thyself for anything, for this is an evidence of the diviner part
within thee being overpowered and yielding to
the less honorable and to the perishable part,
the body, and to its gross pleasures. (IV. 24;
II. 16.)

20. Thy aerial part and all the fiery parts
which are mingled in thee, though by nature they
have an upward tendency, still in obedience to
the disposition of the universe they are overpowered here in the compound mass [the body].
And also the whole of the earthy part in thee
and the watery, though their tendency is down-
ward, still are raised up and occupy a position
which is not their natural one. In this manner
then the elemental parts obey the universal, for
when they have been fixed in any place perforce
they remain there until again the universal shall
sound the signal for dissolution. Is it not then
strange that thy intelligent part only should be
disobedient and discontented with its own place?
And yet no force is imposed on it, but only those
things which are conformable to its nature: still

it does not submit, but is carried in the opposite direction. For the movement towards injustice and intemperance and to anger and grief and fear is nothing else than the act of one who deviates from nature. And also when the ruling faculty is discontented with anything that happens, then too it deserts its post: for it is constituted for piety and reverence towards the gods no less than for justice. For these qualities also are comprehended under the generic term of contentment with the constitution of things, and indeed they are prior [6] to acts of justice.

[6] The word πρεσβύτερα, which is here translated "prior," may also mean "superior:" but Antoninus seems to say that piety and reverence of the gods precede all virtues, and that other virtues are derived from them, even justice, which in another passage (XI. 10) he makes the foundation of all virtues. The ancient notion of justice is that of giving to every one his due. It is not a legal definition, as some have supposed, but a moral rule which law cannot in all cases enforce. Besides law has its own rules, which are sometimes moral and sometimes immoral; but it enforces them all simply because they are general rules, and if it did not or could not enforce them, so far Law would not be Law. Justice, or the doing what is just, implies a universal rule and obedience to it; and as we all live under universal Law, which commands both our body and our intelligence, and is the law of our nature, that is the law of

21. He who has not one and always the same object in life, cannot be one and the same all through his life. But what I have said is not enough, unless this also is added, what this object ought to be. For as there is not the same opinion about all the things which in some way or other are considered by the majority to be good, but only about some certain things, that is, things which concern the common interest; so also ought we to propose to ourselves an object which shall be of a common kind [social] and political. For he who directs all his own efforts to this object, will make all his acts alike, and thus will always be the same.

22. Think of the country mouse and of the town mouse, and of the alarm and trepidation of the town mouse.[7]

23. Socrates used to call the opinions of the many by the name of Lamiae, bugbears to frighten children.

the whole constitution of man, we must endeavour to discover what this supreme Law is. It is the will of the power that rules all. By acting in obedience to this will, we do justice, and by consequence everything else that we ought to do.

[7] The story is told by Horace in his Satires (II. 6), and by others since, but not better.

24. The Lacedaemonians at their public spectacles used to set seats in the shade for strangers, but themselves sat down anywhere.

25. Socrates excused himself to Perdiccas [8] for not going to him, saying, It is because I would not perish by the worst of all ends, that is, I would not receive a favor and then be unable to return it.

26. In the writings of the [Ephesians] [9] there was this precept, constantly to think of some one of the men of former times who practised virtue.

27. The Pythagoreans bid us in the morning look to the heavens that we may be reminded of those bodies which continually do the same things and in the same manner perform their work, and also be reminded of their purity and nudity. For there is no veil over a star.

28. Consider what a man Socrates was when he dressed himself in a skin, after Xanthippe had taken his cloak and gone out, and what Socrates said to his friends who were ashamed of him and drew back from him when they saw him dressed thus.

29. Neither in writing nor in reading wilt thou

[8] Perhaps the emperor made a mistake here, for other writers say that it was Archelaus, the son of Perdiccas, who invited Socrates to Macedonia.

[9] Gataker suggested 'Επικυρείων for 'Εφεσίων.

be able to lay down rules for others before thou
shalt have first learned to obey rules thyself.
Much more is this so in life.

30. A slave thou art: free speech is not for
thee.

31. ——And my heart laughed within. (Od.
ix. 413.)

32. And virtue they will curse speaking harsh
words. (Hesiod, *Works and Days*, 184.)

33. To look for the fig in winter is a madman's
act: such is he who looks for his child when it is
no longer allowed. (Epictetus, iii. 24.)

34. When a man kisses his child, said Epictetus, he should whisper to himself, " To-morrow
perchance thou wilt die " — But those are words
of bad omen — "No word is a word of bad
omen," said Epictetus, " which expresses any
work of nature ; or if it is so, it is also a word
of bad omen to speak of the ears of corn being
reaped." (Epictetus, iii. 24.)

35. The unripe grape, the ripe bunch, the
dried grape, all are changes, not into nothing, but
into something which exists not yet. (Epictetus,
iii. 24.)

36. No man can rob us of our free will.
(Epictetus, iii. 22.)

37. Epictetus also said, a man must discover

an art [or rules] with respect to giving his assent; and in respect to his movements he must
be careful that they be made with regard to circumstances, that they be consistent with social
interests, that they have regard to the value of
the object; and as to sensual desire, he should
altogether keep away from it; and as to avoidance, [aversion] he should not show it with respect to any of the things which are not in our
power.

38. The dispute then, he said, is not about
any common matter, but about being mad or not.

39. Socrates used to say, What do you want?
Souls of rational men or irrational? — Souls of
rational men — Of what rational men? Sound or
unsound? — Sound — Why then do you not seek
for them? — Because we have them — Why then
do you fight and quarrel?

XII.

ALL those things at which thou wishest to arrive by a circuitous road, thou . canst have now, if thou dost not refuse them to thyself. And this means, if thou wilt take no notice of all the past, and trust the future to providence, and direct the present only conformably to piety and justice. Conformably to piety, that thou mayst be content with the lot which is assigned to thee, for nature designed it for thee and thee for it. Conformably to justice, that thou mayst always speak the truth freely and without disguise, and do the things which are agreeable to law and according to the worth of each. And let neither another man's wickedness hinder thee, nor opinion nor voice, nor yet the sensations of the poor flesh which has grown about thee ; for the passive part will look to this. If then, whatever the time may be when thou shalt be near to thy departure, neglecting everything else thou shalt respect only thy

19

ruling faculty and the divinity within thee, and
if thou shalt be afraid not because thou must
some time cease to live, but if thou shalt fear
never to have begun to live according to nature
— then thou wilt be a man worthy of the universe which has produced thee, and thou wilt
cease to be a stranger in thy native land, and to
wonder at things which happen daily as if they
were something unexpected, and to be dependent
on this or that.

2. God sees the minds (ruling principles) of
all men bared of the material vesture and rind
and impurities. With his intellectual part alone
he touches the intelligence only which has flowed
and been derived from himself into these bodies.
And if thou also usest thyself to do this, thou wilt
rid thyself of thy much trouble. For he who
regards not the poor flesh which envelopes him,
surely will not trouble himself by looking after
raiment and dwelling and fame and such like
externals and show.

3. The things are three of which thou art
composed, body, breath [life], intelligence. Of
these the first two are thine, so far as it is thy
duty to take care of them; but the third alone is
properly thine. Therefore if thou shalt separate
from thyself, that is, from thy understanding, what-

ever others do or say, and whatever thou hast
done or said thyself, and whatever future things
trouble thee because they may happen, and whatever in the body which envelopes thee or in the
breath, [life] which is by nature associated with
the body, is attached to thee independent of thy
will, and whatever the external circumfluent vor-
tex whirls round, so that the intellectual power
exempt from the things of fate can live pure and
free by itself, doing what is just and accepting
what happens and saying the truth : if thou wilt
separate, I say, from this ruling faculty the things
which are attached to it by the impressions of
sense, and the things of time to come and of time
that is past, and wilt make thyself like Empedocles' sphere, —

All round, and in its joyous rest reposing ; [1]

and if thou shalt strive to live only what is really
thy life, that is, the present — then thou wilt be
able to pass that portion of life which remains for
thee up to the time of thy death, free from perturbations, nobly, and obedient to thy own daemon
[to the god that is within thee]. (II. 13. 17 ; III.
5, 6 ; XI. 12.)

[1] The verse of Empedocles is corrupt in Antoninus.
It has been restored by Peyron thus :

Σφαῖρος κυκλοτερὴς μονίῃ περιγηθέι γαίων.

4. I have often wondered how it is that every man loves himself more than all the rest of men, but yet sets less value on his own opinion of himself than on the opinion of others. If then a god or a wise teacher should present himself to a man and bid him to think of nothing and to design nothing which he would not express as soon as he conceived it, he could not endure it even for a single day. So much more respect have we to what our neighbors shall think of us than to what we shall think of ourselves.

5. How can it be that the gods after having arranged all things well and benevolently for mankind, have overlooked this alone, that some men and very good men, and men who, as we may say, have had most communion with the divinity, and through pious acts and religious observances have been most intimate with the divinity, when they have once died should never exist again, but should be completely extinguished?

But if this is so, be assured that if it ought to have been otherwise, the gods would have done it. For if it were just, it would also be possible; and if it were according to nature, nature would have had it so. But because it is not so, if in fact it is not so, be thou convinced that it ought not to have been so: — for thou seest even of thyself that in this inquiry thou art disputing with the deity; and we should not thus dispute with the gods, unless they were most excellent and most just; — but if this is so, they would not have allowed anything in the ordering of the universe to be neglected unjustly and irrationally.

6. Practise thyself even in the things which thou despairest of accomplishing. For even the left hand, which is ineffectual for all other things for want of practice, holds the bridle more vigorously than the right hand; for it has been practised in this.

7. Consider in what condition both in body and soul a man should be when he is overtaken by death; and consider the shortness of life, the boundless abyss of time past and future, the feebleness of all matter.

8. Contemplate the formative principles [forms] of things bare of their coverings; the purposes of actions; consider what pain is, what pleasure is, and death, and fame; who is to himself the cause of his uneasiness; how no man is hindered by another; that everything is opinion.

9. In the application of thy principles thou must be like the pancratiast, not like the gladiator; for the gladiator lets fall the sword which he uses and is killed; but the other always has

294 M. ANTONINUS. XII.

his hand, and needs to do nothing else than use it.

10. See what things are in themselves, dividing them into matter, form and purpose.

11. What a power man has to do nothing except what God will approve, and to accept all that God may give him.

12. With respect to that which happens conformably to nature, we ought to blame neither gods, for they do nothing wrong either voluntarily or involuntarily, nor men, for they do nothing wrong except involuntarily. Consequently we should blame nobody. (II. 11, 12, 13; VII. 62; VIII. 17.)

13. How ridiculous and what a stranger he is who is surprised at anything which happens in life.

14. Either there is a fatal necessity and invincible order, or a kind providence, or a confusion without a purpose and without a director. If then there is an invincible necessity, why dost thou resist? But if there is a providence which allows itself to be propitiated, make thyself worthy of the help of the divinity. But if there is a confusion without a governor, be content that in such a tempest thou hast in thyself a certain ruling intelligence. And even if the tempest

carry thee away, let it carry away the poor flesh, the breath, everything else ; for the intelligence at least it will not carry away.

15. Does the light of the lamp shine without losing its splendor until it is extinguished ; and shall the truth which is in thee and justice and temperance be extinguished [before thy death] ?

16. When a man has presented the appearance of having done wrong, [say,] How then do I know if this is a wrongful act? And even if he has done wrong, how do I know that he has not condemned himself? and so this is like tearing his own face. Consider that he, who would not have the bad man do wrong, is like the man who would not have the fig-tree to bear juice in the figs and infants to cry and the horse to neigh, and whatever else must of necessity be. For what must a man do who has such a character? If then thou art irritable,† cure this man's disposition.²

17. If it is not right, do not do it : if it is not true, do not say it. [For let thy efforts be. —]³

18. In everything always observe what the thing is which produces for thee an appearance,

² The interpreters translate γοργός by the words " acer, validusque," and "skilful." But in Epictetus γοργός means " vehement," " prone to anger," " irritable."

³ There is something wrong here, or incomplete.

and resolve it by dividing it into the formal, the material, the purpose, and the time within which it must end.

19. Perceive at last that thou hast in thee something better and more divine than the things which cause the various affects, and as it were pull thee by the strings. What is there now in my mind? is it fear, or suspicion, or desire, or anything of the kind? (v. 11.)

20. First, do nothing inconsiderately, nor without a purpose. Second, make thy acts refer to nothing else than to a social end.

21. Consider that before long thou wilt be nobody and nowhere, nor will any of the things exist which thou now seest, nor any of those who are now living. For all things are formed by nature to change and be turned and to perish in order that other things in continuous succession may exist.

22. Consider that everything is opinion, and opinion is in thy power. Take away then, when thou choosest, thy opinion, and like a mariner, who has doubled the promontory, thou wilt find calm, everything stable, and a waveless bay.

23. Any one activity whatever it may be, when it has ceased at its proper time, suffers no evil because it has ceased; nor he who has done this act,

does he suffer any evil for this reason that the act has ceased. In like manner then the whole which consists of all the acts, which is our life, if it cease at its proper time, suffers no evil for this reason that it has ceased; nor he who has terminated this series at the proper time, has he been ill dealt with. But the proper time and the limit nature fixes, sometimes as in old age the peculiar nature of man, but always the universal nature, by the change of whose parts the whole universe continues ever young and perfect. And everything which is useful to the universal is always good and in season. Therefore the termination of life for every man is no evil, because neither is it shameful, since it is both independent of the will and not opposed to the general interest, but it is good, since it is seasonable and profitable to and congruent with the universal. For thus too he is moved by the deity who is moved in the same manner with the deity and towards the same things in his mind.

24. These three principles thou must have in readiness. In the things which thou doest do nothing either inconsiderately or otherwise than as justice herself would act; but with respect to what may happen to thee from without, consider that it happens either by chance or according to

providence, and thou must neither blame chance nor accuse providence. Second, consider what every being is from the seed to the time of its receiving a soul, and from the reception of a soul to the giving back of the same, and of what things every being is compounded and into what things it is resolved. Third, if thou shouldst suddenly be raised up above the earth, and shouldst look down on human things, and observe the variety of them how great it is, and at the same time also shouldst see at a glance how great is the number of beings who dwell all around in the air and the aether, consider that as often as thou shouldst be raised up, thou wouldst see the same things, sameness of form and shortness of duration. Are these things to be proud of?

25. Cast away opinion: thou art saved. Who then hinders thee from casting it away?

26. When thou art troubled about anything, thou hast forgotten this, that all things happen according to the universal nature; and forgotten this, that a man's wrongful act is nothing to thee; and further thou hast forgotten this, that everything which happens, always happened so and will happen so, and now happens so everywhere; forgotten this too, how close is the kinship between a man and the whole human race, for it is a com-

munity, not of a little blood or seed, but of intelligence. And thou hast forgotten this too, that every man's intelligence is a god, and is an efflux of the deity; and forgotten this, that nothing is a man's own, but that his child and his body and his very soul came from the deity; forgotten this, that everything is opinion; and lastly thou hast forgotten that every man lives the present time only, and loses only this.

27. Constantly bring to thy recollection those who have complained greatly about anything, those who have been most conspicuous by the greatest fame or misfortunes or enmities or fortunes of any kind: then think where are they all now? Smoke and ash and a tale, or not even a tale. And let there be present to thy mind also everything of this sort, how Fabius Catullinus lived in the country, and Lucius Lupus in his gardens, and Stertinius at Baiae, and Tiberius at Capreae and Velius Rufus [or Rufus at Velia]; and in fine think of the eager pursuit of anything conjoined with pride; and how worthless everything is after which men violently strain; and how much more philosophical it is for a man in the opportunities presented to him to show himself just, temperate, obedient to the gods, and to do this with all simplicity: for the pride which is

proud of its want of pride is the most intolerable
of all.

28. To those who ask, Where hast thou seen
the gods or how dost thou comprehend that they
exist and so worshippest them, I answer, in the
first place, they may be seen even with the eyes ; [4]

[4] " Seen even with the eyes." It is supposed that this
may be explained by the Stoic doctrine, that the universe
is a god (IV. 23), and that the celestial bodies are gods
(VIII. 19). But the emperor may mean that we know
that the gods exist, as he afterwards states it, because
we see what they do ; as we know that man has intellectual powers. because we see what he does, and in no other
way do we know it. This passage then will agree with
the passage in the Epistle to the Romans (I. v. 20), and
with the Epistle to the Colossians (I. v. 15), in which
Jesus Christ is named " the image of the invisible
god ; " and with the passage in the Gospel of St. John
(XIV. v. 9).

Gataker, whose notes are a wonderful collection of
learning, and all of it sound and good, quotes a passage
of Calvin which is founded on St. Paul's language (Rom.
I. c. 20) : " God by creating the universe [or world,
mundum], being himself invisible, has presented himself
to our eyes conspicuously in a certain visible form."
He also quotes Seneca (De Benef. IV. c. 8.) : " Quo-
cunque te flexeris, ibi illum videbis occurrentem tibi :
nihil ab illo vacat, opus suum ipse implet." Compare
also Cicero, De Senectute (c. 22), and Xenophon's
Cyropaedia. (VIII. 7.) I think that my interpretation of
Antoninus is right.

in the second place neither have I seen even my own soul and yet I honor it. Thus then with respect to the gods, from what I constantly experience of their power, from this I comprehend that they exist and I venerate them.

29. The safety of life is this, to examine everything all through, what it is itself, what is its material, what its formal part; with all thy soul to do justice and to say the truth. What remains except to enjoy life by joining one good thing to another so as not to leave even the smallest intervals between?

30. There is one light of the sun, though it is distributed over walls, mountains, and other things infinite. There is one common substance, though it is distributed among countless bodies which have their several qualities. There is one soul, though it is distributed among infinite natures and individual circumscriptions [or individuals]. There is one intelligent soul, though it seems to be divided. Now in the things which have been mentioned all the other parts, such as those which are air and substance, are without sensation and have no fellowship: and yet even these parts the intelligent principle holds together and the gravitation towards the same. But intellect in a peculiar manner tends to that which is of the same kin,

and combines with it, and the feeling for communion is not interrupted.

31. What dost thou wish? to continue to exist?
Well, dost thou wish to have sensation? movement? growth? and then again to cease to grow?
to use thy speech? to think? What is there of
all these things which seems to thee worth desiring? But if it is easy to set little value on all
these things, turn to that which remains, which is
to follow reason and god. But it is inconsistent
with honoring reason and god to be troubled because by death a man will be deprived of the
other things.

32. How small a part of the boundless and un-
fathomable time is assigned to every man? for it
is very soon swallowed up in the eternal. And
how small a part of the whole substance? and
how small a part of the universal soul? and on
what a small clod of the whole earth thou creep-
est? Reflecting on all this consider nothing to be
great, except to act as thy nature leads thee, and
to endure that which the common nature brings.

33. How does the ruling faculty make use of
itself? for all lies in this. But everything else,
whether it is in the power of thy will or not, is
only lifeless ashes and smoke.

34. This reflection is most adapted to move us

to contempt of death, that even those who think pleasure to be a good and pain an evil still have despised it.

35. The man to whom that only is good which comes in due season, and to whom it is the same thing whether he has done more or fewer acts conformable to right reason, and to whom it makes no difference whether he contemplates the world for a longer or a shorter time — for this man neither is death a terrible thing. (III. 7; VI. 23; X. 20; XII. 23.)

36. Man, thou hast been a citizen in this great state [the world]: what difference does it make to thee whether for five years [or three]? for that which is conformable to the laws is just for all. Where is the hardship then, if no tyrant nor yet an unjust judge sends thee away from the state, but nature who brought thee into it? the same as if a praetor who has employed an actor dismisses him from the stage — " But I have not finished the five acts, but only three of them " — Thou sayest well, but in life the three acts are the whole drama; for what shall be a complete drama is determined by him who was once the cause of its composition, and now of its dissolution: but thou art the cause of neither. Depart then satisfied, for he also who releases thee is satisfied.

INDEX.

INDEX.

εἶδος, in divisione formae sunt, quas Graeci εἴδη vocant; nostri, si qui haec forte tractant, species appellant (Cic.) But εἶδος is used by Epictetus and Antoninus less exactly and as a general term, like *genus.* Index Epict. ed. Schweigh. — Ὡς δέ γε αἱ πρῶται οὐσίαι πρὸς τὰ ἄλλα ἔχουσιν, οὕτω καὶ τὸ εἶδος πρὸς τὸ γένος ἔχει· ὑπόκειται γὰρ τὸ εἶδος τῷ γένει. (Aristot. Cat. c. 5.)

εἱμαρμένη, (fatalis necessitas, fatum, Cic.), destiny, necessity.

ἐκκλίσεις, aversions, avoidance, the turning away from things ; the opposite of ὀρέξεις.

ἔμψυχα, τά, things which have life.

ἐνέργεια, action, activity.

ἔννοια, ἔννοιαι, notio, notiones (Cic.), or "notitiae rerum;" notions of things. (Notionem appello quam Graeci tum ἔννοιαν, tum πρόληψιν, Cic.)

ἐπιστροφή, attention to an object.

εὐθυμία, animi tranquillitas, (Cic.)

ἡγεμονικόν, τό, the ruling faculty ; principatus, (Cicero.)

θεωρήματα, percepta (Cic.), things perceived, general principles.

καλός, beautiful.

κατάληψις, comprehension ; cognitio, perceptio, comprehensio (Cicero).

κατασκευή, constitution.

κατορθώσεις, κατορθώματα; recta, recte facta (Cicero) ; right acts, those acts to which we proceed by the right or straight road.

κόσμος, order, world, universe.

κόσμος, ὁ ὅλος, the universe, that which is the One and the All, (vi. 25.)

λογικά, τά, the things which have reason.

λογικός, rational.

λόγος, reason.

λόγος σπερματικός, seminal principle.

μέσα, τά, things indifferent, viewed with respect to virtue.

ὕλη, matter, material.

ὑλικόν, τό, the material principle.

ὑπεξαίρεσις, exception, reservation; μεθ᾽ ὑπεξαιρέσεως, conditionally.

ὑπόθεσις, material to work on ; thing to employ the reason on ; proposition, thing assumed as matter for argument and to lead to conclusions. (Quaestionum duo sunt genera; alterum infinitum, definitum alterum. Definitum est, quod ὑπόθεσιν Gracci, nos *causam* : infinitum, quod θέσιν illi appellant, nos *propositum* possumus nominare. Cic. See Aristot. Anal. Post. ɪ. c. 2).

ὑπόληψις, opinion.

ὑπόστασις, basis, substance, being (x. 5). Epictetus has τί τὸ ὑποστατικὸν καὶ οὐσιῶδες.

ὑφίστασθαι, to subsist, to be.

φαντασίαι (visus, Cic.); appearances, thoughts, impressions (visa animi: Gellius, xɪx. 1) : φαντασία, ἐστὶ τύπωσις ἐν ψυχῇ.

φάντασμα, seems to be used by Antoninus in the same sense as φαντασία. Epictetus uses only φαντασία.

φανταστόν, that which produces a φαντασία : φανταστὸν τὸ πεποιηκὸς τὴν φαντασίαν αἰσθητόν.

φύσις, nature.

φύσις, ἡ τῶν ὅλων, the nature of the universe.

ψυχή, soul, life, living principle.

ψυχὴ λογική, νοερά, a rational soul, an intelligent soul.

THE END.

www.ingramcontent.com/pod-product-compliance
Lightning Source LLC
Chambersburg PA
CBHW031402270326
41929CB00010BA/1293